Matchlines for Singles

HOW TO FIND YOUR PERFECT MATCH!

By

DR. MOLLY BARROW

BARRINGER PUBLISHING
Naples

Published by Barringer Publishing, Inc. January 2010
Cover, graphics, layout design by Barringer Publishing
Editing by Lynne Nolan, M. Ed., Elizabeth Heath, and James A. Barrow

ISBN: 978-0-9825109-2-6

Library of Congress Cataloging-in-Publication Data
Barrow, Molly
Matchlines for Singles/ by Dr. Molly Barrow

Summary: Psychological self-help to improve the selection of a compatible partner, balance existing relationships, build self-esteem and learn assertiveness skills with Matchlines, an original theory of relationships that helps to creates harmony and happiness.

[1. Psychology-Nonfiction. 2. Relationships-Nonfiction. 3. Self-esteem-Psychology. 4. Title]

Printed in U.S.A.

BOOKS BY DR. MOLLY BARROW

RELATIONSHIP SELF-HELP:

Matchlines for Singles

Matchlines Workbook for Couples

Matchlines How to Survive Step Parenting

Matchlines Shrink about This: Chronicles from the Couch

Matchlines A Revolutionary New Way of Looking At Relationships and Making the Right Choices in Love

Pathways and Pitfalls of Co-Parenting after the Divorce (Dissertation)

CHILDREN'S SELF-ESTEEM ADVENTURE SERIES:

Malia and Teacup Awesome African Adventure

Malia and Teacup Out on a Limb

Malia and Teacup Kingdom of the Thunder Dragon

"When a true Matchline comes into your life—and he or she will come—the reward of a healthy, loving, stable relationship is worth the wait."

—Dr. Molly Barrow

Matchlines

f♥r

Singles

HOW TO FIND
YOUR PERFECT MATCH!

CONTENTS

PART 4
LINE LENGTHENING

PART 5
LINES OF COMMUNICATION

PART 6
FINISH LINE

Part 1

MATCHLINE THEORY

"And think not you can direct the course of love, for love, if it finds you worthy, directs your course."

—**Kahlil Gibran**

Chapter 1
THE STARTING LINE

At a romantic, candlelit corner table in an intimate restaurant, my husband and I were delighted to be alone. The restaurant owner appeared with a flushed face. He apologized for the interruption, and then explained that he absolutely had to thank me.

"You drew those Matchlines for me a while back, and you know what? It worked," he said, pulling his new wife over to meet me. "Dinner is on me," he declared, before returning to his place at the front of the restaurant to greet other patrons.

My husband looked at me quizzically, asking, "So what exactly are Matchlines?"

"Techniques that I've developed to help people pick the right mate," I answered. "It's a graphic way to understand love, why it works and why it fails."

After a short silence, he looked over at the restaurant owner, at the lovely dinner, then at me.

I told him, "I waited a long time for a Matchline like you to enter my life."

"What's a Matchline?" he asked suspiciously.

I drew the "Lines" for him on a scrap of paper. As he studied the lines that revealed relationship dynamics, comprehension flashed in his expression. I knew that look. I have shown hundreds of my patients these "Lines." My patients wore that exact same expression when suddenly they understood why they have won or lost at love. They finally saw how loving someone to his or her fullest potential could be achieved.

Is your Line shorter or longer than your partner's Line?

- Does your Line equal the Line of your partner?

- Does your Line or does your partner's Line have a nasty break or fracture from trauma?

- Can a shorter Line ever fulfill a Longline?

- How long were the Lines of Mother Teresa, Marilyn Monroe or your parents?

- Why does a loving, caring, giving and worthy person often lose in the game of love to an obviously less capable person?

The answers are explained in Matchlines for Singles.

LOVE CAPACITY GRAPH

10
9
8
7
6
5
4
3
2
1

WE ALL HAVE DIFFERENT CAPACITIES

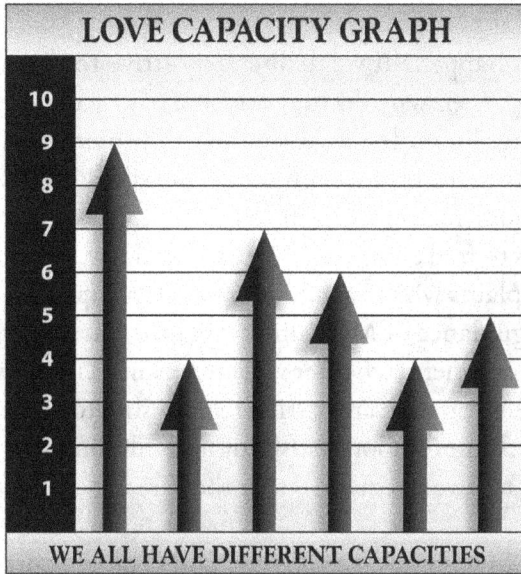

Every person has his own unique Line based upon his ability or capacity to give and receive love. The single most important factor in finding and maintaining a quality love relationship is balancing any differences between the couple's two "Lines."

Frequently, one partner who is seemingly doing all the right, loving things, may unconsciously ruin the relationship. Some people unwittingly love their partners to distraction and end up driving them straight into the loving arms of a rival.

Why does this happen? If we deliberately strive to make our interactions happy and loving, then why do they backfire? Why does one person leave a partner who brings boundless love, support and energy to a relationship?

Once you see the effects of Matchlines Analysis, you will have a new vision of how to help your relationships be successful. Matchlines techniques can give you the tools to find compatible partners and to save quality relationships.

Matchlines explains why some of your relationships may have not worked in the past. The guidance of Matchlines will give you a fighting chance in the matchmaking department, whether you are seeking a new loving relationship, or need tips to help you with an existing relationship to make it more balanced and healthy. Matchlines is about satisfying and fulfilling love relationships and teaches you how to love partners so that they are content and feel free to love you back.

The theory of Matchlines is explained and explored through easy-to-read graphic diagrams. You will be able to graph your own Relationship Capacity Line and estimate the Line of an existing or potential partner. You will discover what happens when certain types of Lines interact.

Matchlines can help to set rocky relationships on a more tranquil course and demonstrates how the route to a more intimate connection with the one you love follows the course of two Lines, not just one.

A MATCHLINE IS THE MISSION

Whatever the actual length of your Relationship Capacity Line, your mission is to find an appropriate match for you with a Line that is not much longer or much shorter than yours is. The Lines do not have to be equal to have a harmonious relationship; however, a Matchline occurs when your Relationship Capacity Line closely matches your partner's Relationship Capacity Line. The goal is to avoid a big difference or Line Gap between your Lines.

Is it better to be a Longline? For the most part, yes, only in the sense that Longlines have a greater capacity to give love and receive love. Longlines are less common, and Shortlines are more plentiful. That is because life tends to kick the openness and trust out of most people, and, as a result, our defenses go up and our Relationship Capacity Lines shorten. All children begin as Longlines. However, very few of us successfully make it through a lifetime with our innocence and openness intact.

You do not need to find an absolutely *perfect* Matchline to find happiness. Your Relationship Capacity Line does not always remain exactly the same length. As life impacts us, our ability to love freely compresses and lengthens as we grieve and then recover from life's losses or disasters. Sometimes we are deeply in love; sometimes we are a little bored. Then slowly we are in love again. A swaying and fluctuating dance is normal and gradual, as evidenced by couples with thirty and forty years of marriage together.

Everyone deserves love and happiness. With Matchlines Analysis, you will discover key balancing techniques that will help you and your partner become the right Matchline for each other.

"All love that has not friendship for its base is
like a mansion built upon the sand."

—Ella Wheeler Wilcox

Chapter 2
THE LINE GAP

Someone who dedicates his or her life's work to ministering to others is an example of someone with a very long Line, because there seems to be no limit to his or her ability to give love. A heartless taker is a likely example of someone with a very short Relationship Capacity Line, capable of little else but perpetual selfishness, and not able to give in a love relationship. The rest of us all have Relationship Capacity Lines that are charted somewhere in-between these extremes.

Relationship Capacity Lines are precisely this: A plotted line representing your ability to give and receive love. Both your inherited and learned love capacity contributes to your Line. The importance of your Relationship Capacity Line is that a truly successful relationship requires Lines that balance to create a Matchline.

Few can imagine the capacity for love and self-sacrifice that it takes to devote your entire life to ministering to desperately poor people. A true Longline is way above the norm. Everyone else can only give what reserves of compassion and energy that he or she has to give.

Between the obvious extremes of an absolute, unconditional, self-sacrificing capacity to love, and an utter selfish lack of any capacity to love, rests the fundamental concept of Matchlines. One Line length does not reflect a more valuable or worthy partner than another. The difference or Line Gap between the two lines of partners is important, not as competition with each other, but essential to knowing how you can make each other more comfortable in the relationship.

The key is this: the difference between your Line and your partner's Line—the **Line Gap**—must be very slight to enjoy easy happiness in a love relationship. When lines are mismatched, people must work harder to keep a relationship **balanced.** If you are the Longline in the relationship, then the responsibility for establishing and maintaining that balance is mostly up to you. The actual level of your Line only matters in determining a compatible match for you. Matchlines Analysis helps you to find true compatible love—not to judge or label anyone as good or bad based upon the length of his or her Relationship Capacity Line. Shortlines are wonderful people, too. They just react differently than Longlines do in a relationship.

Relationship Capacity Lines are precisely this: A plotted line representing your ability to give and receive love. Both your inherited and learned love capacity contributes to your Line. The importance of your Relationship Capacity Line is that a truly successful relationship requires Lines that balance to create a Matchline.

You may be a Longline or a Shortline in an existing relationship, depending on whether the other person in the relationship has more or less capacity to love than you. You may think you are a Longline in general, compared to all people, however, if your partner's Relationship Capacity Line is longer than yours, then you become the Shortline in that relationship. The power of Matchlines is to illustrate a "relative" relationship between two people—never an absolute judgment about anyone's value as a person.

You will benefit from thoroughly assessing your relationships, past and present, to determine your Line Gaps, or differences, with respect to your past partners (or a potential partner). This information will reveal whether or not you relate to your companion in the ideal way, according to Matchlines Analysis.

I REALLY LOVE YOU

When Longlines use the word "love," their definition of that word includes their entire experience of love since their earliest childhood. Unfortunately, Shortlines use the exact same word, "love," but their experience of love may bear no resemblance whatsoever to the Longlines' definition of love. This is where understanding the dynamics of a large Gap between the Lines in a relationship begins.

Shortlines may have experienced less nurturing and affection in life, and/or possess a history of pain and neglect mixed into their very earliest memories. When a person loves you, he or she is giving you the best love he knows how to give. Your partner is giving all that he or she is currently capable of giving regardless of whether you find those efforts satisfactory or unsatisfactory, fulfilling or disappointing. This is the fundamental secret in understanding the concept of finding balance between two distinctly different Lines in a relationship.

We cannot see beyond our past, our experience, our personal limits or beyond the end of our Line. We each have a **Line Ceiling.** Quite often, Shortlines know very little about the kind of love that is sky high and limitless, unconditional and genuinely passionate—the kind of love that Longlines are more capable of giving and receiving and tend to **expect in return.** For the Shortline, possible past trauma or neglect can form an internal "ceiling," which inhibits them and obscures emotional heights. Shortlines have great difficulty seeing above their personal ceiling to meet the needs of the Longlines—and that is the crux of many problems in such a relationship.

Shortlines are giving as much love as they have to give, all they perceive love to be. They do not think about the qualities of love beyond the confines of their own Ceiling. This limited vision inhibits their ability to love beyond the length or capacity of their Line. Each of us is limited by our own Line Ceiling.

LOVE CAPACITY GRAPH

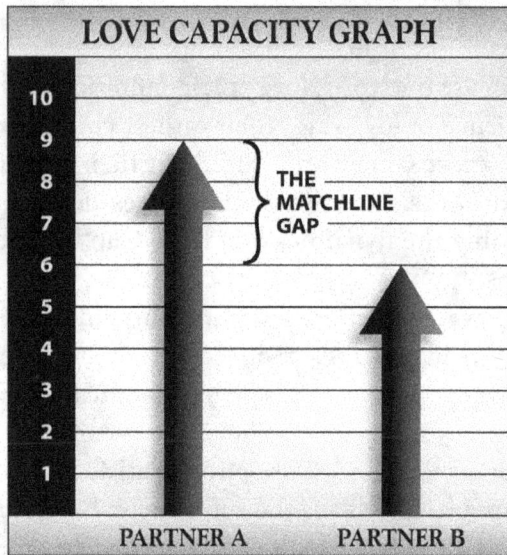

THE MATCHLINE GAP

PARTNER A   PARTNER B

The difference between your Line and your partner's Line—the **Line Gap**—must be very slight to enjoy easy happiness in a love relationship. When lines are mismatched, people must work harder to keep a relationship balanced.

♥

I Love You This Much

When someone tells you that he loves you, what he truly means is his (not your) definition and understanding of love to the extent of his Line Ceiling, but never beyond it. Your partner's definition of love is only as high as his Ceiling allows him to love. Your partner gives you what he or she can. He is not withholding love—despite what you may feel. He simply does not have the capacity to give you more of what you need and want. He has restrictions from his childhood and current behavior. He may lack relationship experience and comprehension compared to a Longline.

If you are the Longline in a relationship, the concept of a Shortline is not meant to be an excuse for your partner's genuine displays of selfishness. Lines are to help you understand the real reasons why some people just don't have the same capacity to give and receive love as others—even when they, themselves, sincerely believe they are doing a great job loving you. Remember, a Shortline is giving the best love that he possibly can.

The size of the Line Gap, not the existence of one, makes or breaks relationships. The important point to focus on is determining the extent of the Line Gap between you and an existing or potential partner. If the Line Gap is small, love will be easier for you both. If the Line Gap is great, finding a harmonious love will be harder. Unfortunately, Line Gaps are common, but the good news is that the better you understand them, and their effects on you as a couple, the easier the work to balance a relationship will be for you and your partner.

This Line Gap represents fundamental behavior differences that have the ability to create constant friction, conflict, disappointment and frustration. Resolving Line Gap problems is usually hard work, and sometimes in worst case situations, when the Line Gap is just too far apart, may even be impossible to balance. Line Gaps exist in successful relationships, conflicted relationships, relationships with your family members, and even with your boss. The Line Gap is in every relationship. Balancing the Line Gap is the challenge and goal of all your relationship efforts. **The Line Gap is the most significant relationship consideration.**

If you are the Longline in a relationship, then think of your Shortline partner as someone who is emotionally more numb or distant in most circumstances than you are because they have been hurt more. Imagine a cut that even when healed may have tough scar tissue protectively remaining and lessening sensitivity. Shortlines' emotional defenses diminish their ability and openness to meeting the needs of others. They have more difficulty establishing a close, trusting and loving relationship than a longer Line does. Shortlines have less control over the factors that affect them, and react differently than Longlines within their respective Line ceilings. Consequently, a Shortline's approach to giving and receiving emotional intimacy will differ from the approach of the longer Line in a relationship.

Longlines are more prone to share intimate feelings openly and actively seek the understanding and support of their partners. Conversely, because Shortlines' needs for close companionship and emotional intimacy are either less accessible or simply less than Longlines' needs, Shortlines can completely satisfy their needs with less investment of time or energy.

Think of this concept in terms of a person's appetite for food and nourishment, predicated on the physical capacity of their stomach—that is, how much they can actually hold. How much do they need to eat in a given meal to feel full? When a person with a smaller appetite eats a little, he soon feels full and satisfied and does not want any more to eat. However, his partner, who may have a much larger appetite, may get his feelings hurt when halfway through his own meal he sees his smaller appetite partner push away from the table and stop eating. The Longline is left wondering if it is because his or her cooking or company is bad—when neither was the case at all.

At first, Shortlines may not feel the existence of the Line Gap, perhaps obliviously and frustratingly so for the Longlines, but Longlines surely will feel it. Feeling content themselves, Shortlines are typically completely unaware of Line Gaps and the resulting unmet needs of their Longline partners. The inevitable result in this situation is that Shortlines unintentionally starve Longlines of intimacy, and Longlines invariably overstuff and suffocate Shortlines.

CROSSED LINES

Shortline says to Longline: *"I love you."*

Shortline means: *"I think you're pretty hot and we get along fine."*

Longline hears: *"I love you and want to spend the rest of my life with you and get married and have babies and live in a house and travel the world and drive a minivan and never leave you lonely, ever, ever, again!"*

Since Shortlines cannot see beyond the top of their own Matchlines Ceiling, they often fail to realize that an intimacy potential may exist beyond what merely fulfills them. They cannot imagine that their partner needs more, or that "more" exists other than what they have experienced in their lifetime. Nevertheless, Shortlines' efforts are one hundred percent of their ability. The Longline must therefore always remember that the Shortline partner is doing **all** he or she can to love the Longline—even if it is not enough.

"One word frees us of all the weight and pain in life. That word is love."

—Sophocles

Chapter 3
LONELY LONGLINES

As time passes, Longlines' needs remain only partially met. Longlines feel the Line Gap acutely in the form of dull, aching loneliness. Despite trying to love their partners to the best of their ability, the relationship feels unsatisfying. On the other hand, Shortlines are content until Longlines begin to ask for more—more time, more attention, more commitment, more fun, more foreplay and more intimacy. The message from the Longline to the Shortline is loud and clear: The Shortline is not providing enough.

From the Shortline's perspective, the "excessive" needs of the Longline become nagging and tiresome. If the Line Gaps are extensive, then well-meaning and genuinely loving Longlines will ultimately suffer deeply from unsatisfied, unrequited, emotional hunger and neglect.

Eventually, Shortlines only hear the perpetual drumbeat of "you are not good enough" in every request for more. Because Shortlines misunderstand the Longlines' cry of need as nasty criticism, they harshly react to the annoying Longline with rejection. Shortlines want less than Longlines—less love, less closeness, less intimacy and become frustrated with anyone who bothers them for "more." The attempt to force feed intimacy when they are already full is similar to offering a second Thanksgiving dinner right after the first! Even something this wonderful is repulsive when it is too much.

CROSSED LINES

> **Longline says to Shortline:** *"I wish you were more affectionate."*
>
> **Longline means:** *"I love you and I'm trying to tell you in a nice way, without making you angry or defensive or scared, that I wish you would pay more attention to me."*
>
> **Shortline hears:** *"I am unhappy in this relationship, you are not a good enough partner for me and you are not meeting my needs, so change."*

The satiated Shortline naturally withdraws from the Longline's demands and criticism, born out of anxiety and discomfort. In time, Shortlines start to avoid any interaction with their Longline partners—simply for the peace and quiet!

STARVED FOR AFFECTION

Just as naturally, needy Longlines begin to escalate their efforts to alleviate the pain of their emotional starvation by begging, whining, nagging and complaining. Longlines seem increasingly unappealing to the already retreating Shortlines. Withdrawals are soon painfully obvious. The Longline, in turn, panics and tries even harder to keep their Shortline close, while the Shortline continues to back away.

Frustrated by this constant pressure, Shortlines begin making up excuses to avoid the oppression. Do any of these common excuses sound familiar?

"I was with you last night."

"I need time with my friends."

"I have to work late."

"I need some space."

"I want to be alone."

Longlines feel this rejection and respond by doing what they do best—to offer more love, compassion and understanding in an urgent, clinging way that, in their mind, is supposed to draw a partner closer.

As Longlines continue to push and shove their version of love into the overstuffed Shortlines, Shortlines can be expected to react by striking out viciously, just to get some breathing room. In this co-dependent dance, Shortlines bend away from Longlines as Longlines intrude increasingly into the personal space of the Shortline. Each partner is attempting to manipulate the relationship imbalance to find his or her level of relationship comfort and balance. This reaction to the differences in each partner's needs is ineffective. Rather than enable the relationship to thrive, this pattern has the opposite result. Feelings of resentment will eventually replace feelings of love.

SURELY *THIS* PERSON WILL WANT ME

Longlines are often left alone in a relationship, or forsaken because they give too much of a good thing. Unfortunately, chronically rejected Longlines will mistakenly either cling to the dying relationship, or seek out, in a state of plummeting self-esteem, an **even less desirable match.** Longlines hope that their new, even shorter Line partner will surely value them better than their last partner did. Most new relationships start out fun, hot, exciting and tender because they are new. However, the pitfalls of even larger emotional Line Gaps will soon begin to take effect in these new relationships as well, just like before, in a never-ending, downward-spiraling cycle—unless some fundamental **changes** in perspective and behavior are introduced into the equation.

Once Longlines understand some of the intricacies of Matchlines Analysis, then they can make better choices to avoid the downward, spiraling cycle and restore their self-esteem. If this pattern sounds all-too-familiar in your own experience, do not despair; there is hope. Soon, you will be able to recognize quickly the length of another's Line from a safe distance, long before you get hurt, and can still say "no" to the relationship. Instead of over-loving your partner out the door, you can learn to love your partner the way he or she needs to be loved.

CROSSED LINES

Longline says: *"Love me, love my children, my cat, my dog and my mother."*

Shortline says: *"Love me, reject all others."*

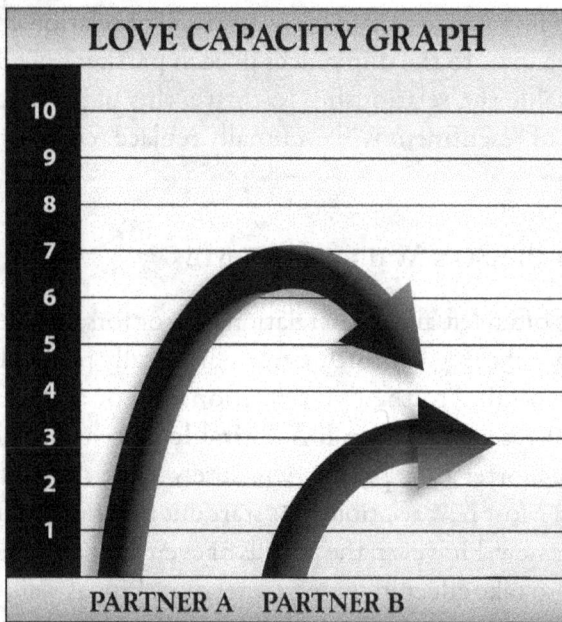

LOVE CAPACITY GRAPH

10	
9	
8	
7	
6	
5	
4	
3	
2	
1	

PARTNER A   PARTNER B

In this co-dependent dance, Shortlines bend away from Longlines as Longlines intrude increasingly into the personal space of the Shortline.

ARE YOU A LONGLINE?

How does the length of our Line develop, and how can we gauge where we stand in our most important personal relationships? Is the length of our Line a function of heredity or a result of the way we were nurtured? While the ability to give and receive love may not be a genetic trait, your parents are a very important consideration in answering this question. Parents have an impact of both nature (parents' genes) and nurture (childhood events and treatment.)

"*Tell me whom you love and I will tell you who
you are.*"

—Houssaye

Chapter 4
YOUR LINEAGE

*M*uch like many other aspects of your personality, intellect and character, your Line is established and functioning by the time that you reach your adolescent years. In many respects, your Line is the result of a long string of key variables—from the way that your parents raised you, to how, as an adult, you view yourself and the world around you. Just as every individual on the planet is different from the next, so is each person's Line unique. Nevertheless, people clearly reveal fundamental patterns in their behavior and past relationships that you can easily observe and measure.

As children, we begin perfectly in the emotional arena, innocent and eager, although we completely lack learned socialization skills. Our experiences and our environment mold us. The experiences of our parents and their environment also subtly influence us. Parents pass down their fears and prejudices to us just as their genes are passed to us. However, unlike eye color, you can change opinions.

In the lab, pigeons repeat their behavior when they receive a food pellet or reward. Learned behavior when accompanied by rewards is called "conditioning." In humans, because of childhood nurturing, or the lack of it, learned needs develop along with a learned capability to meet those needs. The learned needs, or lack of them, help to create a person's Relationship

Capacity Line. **All behavior we express is either reinforced positively (praise, a smile, a dollar) or negatively (criticism, punishment, lack of attention, abuse), or else it fades away.**

In essence, the bulk of what we individually define as "love" is a truly learned behavior. Your parents, grandparents, other relatives, friends, neighbors, teachers, coaches, clergy, books, television, movies, plays, games, songs and a host of other influences all contribute to your personal definition of love.

What was love to you as a child? Was love being read a story at night as you fell asleep? Was love demonstrated by a big hug and a kiss, or were your parents less capable of giving affection? Maybe your parent substituted quality time with material things, like a new bicycle, a game, or a box of cookies. Perhaps they left you alone too much, or gave you damaging attention that made you believe love is someone who says you are not competent or that you deserve harsh treatment.

Your personal definition of love primarily stems from learning that took place before you were ten years old and subsequently became part of your core belief system. You cannot easily change your belief system. It is like the concrete foundation of your psyche. The main point here to understand is that your personal definition of love may be a world apart from your partner's definition. Yes, your partner may say that he or she loves you, but is it your kind of love? When you give love, is it your partner's kind of love?

BLOODLINES

Now let us look at the genetic, hereditary side of the equation. If you examine the bloodlines of purebred animals, you soon realize that a winner is no accident. Through carefully selected breeding, prized racehorses, champion show dogs and blue ribbon cattle have the most superior gene traits that money can buy. Usually, we discover that the champion's parents were also champions.

If a Greyhound sire has a genetic hip problem, this trait may or may not show up in the next generation. However, you cannot make the recurring genetic hip problem go away, regardless of how much you love the dog or train it. The hip is weak, if only in potential to fail. You would not bet your life or finances on that particular dog winning a race, or that its puppies will be free from hip problems. The dog's effort may be one hundred percent. The result could still be beneath your expectations or a complete failure.

That does not mean the injured dog cannot be loved, and love its owner in return. However, if the owner ties his love of the dog to the dog winning a race (a specific expected behavior), then that dog's performance may come up short. If the owner is aware of the shortcomings and loves the dog anyway that is a knowledgeable informed choice and is the owner's right. Rather, it is the unknown surprise or denial of obvious truth that can be so damaging. This is why it is crucial to know any potential partner's Line.

Psychologists hotly debate just which aspects of human behavior might be purely genetic in origin. Predispositions to certain weaknesses or strengths or to differing aspects of a person's character, such as stubbornness or a good sense of humor could be learned behavior. Nevertheless, we directly inherit some physical attributes from parents. Being tall or short, big-boned or delicate, good or bad eyesight, nervous or calm, brilliant or not, straight teeth or crooked teeth, etc., can have an impact on a person's self-esteem and self-confidence, especially for a child growing up and dealing with critical peer groups.

By examining the bloodlines of you and your partner, you will gain insight and tools to recognize family traits, strengths and weaknesses. Generational information will help to determine the differences between your Lines— information that will help you to find a balanced path that leads to a healthy, loving relationship with that person.

SECOND-HAND TRAUMA

If you are the Longline in a relationship with a Shortline, perhaps an extreme Shortline, then you must come to understand and accept certain truths of your situation. Despite your most fervent hopes and desires to the contrary, a person with a history of deep emotional childhood trauma cannot be "restored" by your excessive love-smothering attention.

Perhaps you must learn to accept the Shortline as he or she is right now, even though an individual can alter many behaviors if he or she chooses to do so. If someone dedicates himself or herself to change, he or she can make great progress. You can be supportive in that process, but you cannot make it happen for him or her. In some cases, emotional doors in people's minds have closed shut and may not ever open again.

People like this might be unfortunate victims who reflect the tragic damage that is often imposed upon children, either maliciously or accidentally, by adults and circumstances. Right now, this person simply does not have the same capacity to love you as someone whose parents loved him or her greatly as a child and who remains free of trauma and abuse as an adult. During a weak moment of high stress, or after one drink too many, the trauma may resurface, and the result may be hurt feelings or abuse for you.

If in your compassion you choose to have a committed love relationship with a person whose Line is substantially shorter than yours is, or possibly even dysfunctional, then you may inevitably become a victim to your partner's trauma-based inadequacies. As surely as second-hand smoke pollutes the air, your partner's past can poison your life, too. Yet, people can change their behavior patterns when they are **self-motivated** and determined to do so. In fact, some people have demonstrated remarkable ability to overcome childhood traumas and the damage of their pasts often with proper professional help, counseling and guidance.

Severely abusive or neglectful caretakers teach their unfortunate victim that the experience of abuse is "normal." As adults, these victims outwardly attempt to reject their harsh training. They may layer over these learned and internalized lessons a sincere desire never to be like their abusers. Most rebound and never repeat their childhood terrors on another generation. However, some flashback and strike out. The childhood conditioning lingers, waiting for a trigger or enough pressure to push all the wrong buttons. What feels "normal" to them may be intolerable treatment to their partners.

In other instances, some people are missing correct and effective socialization techniques needed to interact with others normally. They do not operate within established societal constructs. Compared to most Longlines, their knowledge and experience are severely limited or become skewed. They may have learned only to stay alive at any cost. They might never learn the finer points of how to care for loved ones beyond their own early survival skills, which makes it extremely difficult for them to learn how to be genuine lovers or good parents. They may have the desire for sex, but not friendship. They may want you around, but are unable to treat you nicely.

Sadly, the fundamental concepts of love, kindness, generosity, compassion, parenting, sacrifice, loyalty or friendship are unknown or only partially attained. Many people simply have not honed the rather complicated mechanisms of emotion within themselves. In a sense, they have shut down.

People who have the longest Lines usually are a result of responsible and kindly parenting. Children who escaped damaging childhood trauma are open and eager for close relationships. In the absence of physical or emotional abuse or neglect, nurtured children tend to grow up loving, trusting, ready and willing to give others help, love, and friendship. People who reach adulthood with minimum emotional damage become the longest of all Relationship Capacity Lines.

WHY NOT FORGET THE PAST?

Is bringing up the past necessary in understanding your own Line and the Line of an existing or potential partner? *Absolutely!* In fact, it is one of the key factors in determining and understanding the length of your Line and that of your partner. By examining various aspects and facets of your mother and father, and other influences, you will learn your own capacity to give and receive love.

Were your parents kind, intelligent and nurturing to you? Alternatively, were they selfish and non-socialized, indulging themselves with addictions? Maybe, like most people, were they somewhere in-between?

Can you remember your grandparents and their relationship? Were they disciplinarians, who parented with a strict rod on your dad's back? Perhaps your father passed his childhood rage down to his children. If so, then you may be experiencing a problem in your current relationship that originated with Grandpa, and is now alive and well inside your own definition of love. Remember, your relationship behavior arises from your learned belief system, which reflects your emotional heritage gleaned from past treatment and experience, just as your eye color reflects the gene traits passed on to you by your parents.

Therefore, in selecting a potential spouse or long-term relationship partner, you cannot ignore your partner's emotional heritage any more than you would ignore physical issues such as hemophilia or any other inherited physical malady. You may voluntarily choose to live with any problems or situations. However, at a minimum, you have a right and an obligation to your happiness and your future children to make an informed assessment before you are married or commit to a life partner.

Everything from your partner's entire past influences his or her choices and behavior today, and tomorrow. As you answer the following questions, think about how your family may have influenced the length of your own Relationship Capacity Line.

- Did your parents love you? Did your parents love each other?
- Did they openly show one another affection with hugs, smiles and kisses?
- Did they make holidays and birthdays special events?
- Did they try to keep disagreements contained?
- Did they praise each other and support projects, careers and hobbies?
- Did your parents openly show you their affection, and support you in school, sports and friendships?
- Did they take their time to explain fair disciplinary actions?
- Did a family member ever mistreat the family pet?
- Did you share belly laughs with your parents?
- Did your parents abuse drugs or alcohol?
- Do you remember your grandparents?
- When you visited your grandparents, did they openly show their affection for both you and your parents?
- Were your parents hurtful or distant to each other?
- Do you treat children the way your parents treated you?

You Do Not Have To Be Perfect

Emotional perfection is neither the goal nor the standard anyone can expect of another human being. People may have all sorts of glitches in their lives that are routinely exposed and compensated for in healthy ways. Perhaps your partner refuses to watch the movie Deliverance because of his or her own abuse as a child. If your partner explains this, you can pick another movie and both enjoy the evening. Compare this with a different scenario where your partner says nothing about his or her personal secret, and, halfway through the movie, your partner has an emotional meltdown—he or she hits you, throws a vase and gets drunk. You are stunned and wonder what you did wrong. In the first scenario, that couple is coping openly and constructively with glitches and certain limitations, while the other couple is dysfunctional.

Bad things do happen to good people. That is real life. Yet, just because you may have experienced a significant trauma in your life does not necessarily preclude you from ever becoming a Longline partner—it may be harder, but not impossible. People who have known severe hardship and trauma can still develop into Longlines if someone, somewhere, loved them **unconditionally** as a child.

With unconditional love, children learn to love and give unselfishly in spite of negative impacts or even severely traumatic events. Oprah Winfrey faced very difficult challenges as a child, yet grew up to be a dynamic businessperson and a generous giver to millions of television viewers. Mother Theresa lost her father when she was eight years old, and her mother worked long hours to feed the family. Mother Theresa still grew up to be one of the biggest givers of our time. Abraham Lincoln had an abusive father, and, yet, he was a loving father to his children. In order to lengthen an adult Line, love and acceptance must come from within the individual rather than from other people.

Therefore, to begin to understand another person, it is first important to understand and assess yourself. Only after you have honestly determined the length of your own Line—your inherited and learned love capacity—is it time for you to do a little digging into your partner's past and see how your two Lines match.

"Love is the flower of life, and blossoms unexpectedly and without law, and must be plucked where it is found, and enjoyed for the brief hour of its duration."

—D. H. Lawrence

Chapter 5
DRAW THE LINE

People with very long Lines tend to be like big, adoring golden retriever puppies that wag their tails, crawl on your lap and lick you. People with shorter Lines are more like cats that prefer to sit in a distant corner of the room. If you rush over to a cat, it will be gone before you get there. If you wait patiently, ignoring the cat, it will creep over tentatively and jump in your lap. Is your partner more like a dog, or a cat? Which are you?

If you are the Longline in your relationship, and do not have a cat, then you may want to spend some time with a cat and practice waiting patiently for it to come to you. Tell yourself that you are playing with the cat while you read your favorite book. If you run around the room trying to get a cat to play catch with you, then you are doomed to failure.

The point of this analogy is to help you begin to understand yourself and your partner in a brand new way, based upon behavior patterns.

BASE LINES SCORING

How long can Relationship Capacity Lines be? There is no set dimension to try to achieve because the effect of your Line length only matters **in relation** to your companion's length. The Line Gap is all that is relevant.

Once you have analyzed your own heritage and experience, you can determine your base Line and make strong conclusions with your newfound self-knowledge. After you analyze your partner's Relationship Capacity Line, you will discover who is longer, both overall and in specific areas, and that is the secret to knowing how to treat your partner in a healthy, successful relationship.

You can use the **Matchlines Compatibility Quiz** on www.drmollybarrow.com to help you determine the length of your Line. For now, in a general sense, you can score your Line based on the emotional bloodlines of your parents (or your guardians) and the quality of the relationship they had when you were a child. Extend your Line if you had additional relatives or an influential mentor (in addition to both parents) who loved you unconditionally and dependably when you were less than ten years old. If you escaped trauma and abuse, extend your line a great deal. If you are happy with your physical appearance and accomplishments, extend your Line more. This roughly describes the highest potential for the length of your Relationship Capacity Line.

Many factors can shorten the length of a Line. For example, addiction, overwork, and even too many obligations can shrink the capability of a person to nurture a relationship. Some Lines have serious damage from trauma, abuse or neglect that may cause a relationship to be problematic, if not completely dysfunctional. For now, chart your heritage. Later, you will adjust your Line as you learn more.

Parents like fictional Ward and June Cleaver in Leave It to Beaver demonstrated gentle loving parenting, the kind that helps to produce the longest Relationship Capacity Lines.

Parents who were less nurturing, yet consistent and present, have moderate length Relationship Capacity Lines. Even though they were slightly "shut down" emotionally, they meant well.

Parents, who are severely substance addicted or behaviorally addicted and not in recovery, have difficulty demonstrating real love. Their primary allegiance is to their addiction. If this describes one or both of your parents, or if they abused you, or suffered mental illness, they would go much lower on the chart.

You may have had an alcoholic parent whom you loved try to act lovingly toward you, yet he or she failed you, hurt you or disappointed you. Relationships with a severely addicted person are filled with pretense. Real love is available, committed, dependable, sacrificing and plentiful. Alcoholic or addicted love often contains empty promises: "I am going to..." only words, followed by excuses. Meanwhile, you are doing all the work in the relationship, and you often settle for less in return than you are giving. For some people any criticism of their parents may be a hard idea to accept. You have little opportunity to help a parent overcome the early traumas of his or her life. However, this is your chance at a good life. It is important for you to recognize those areas in your life that may have been damaging or improperly modeled in the past, and therefore need work, or possibly even professional help in order to heal from them.

Many events from the past can shorten your Line, such as sexual abuse, abandonment or overwhelming loss. Chemical addictions, such as alcohol and drugs, or behavioral addictions, like excessive spending, gambling, pornography or theft of any kind, are usually destructive in a relationship, and therefore, can cut your Relationship Capacity Line severely.

Lines scoring near the very bottom of the chart reflect relationships that are less about love and compatibility and more about survival; but these relationships can work well with a closely matched partner versed in Matchlines Balancing. Two well-matched, very short Lines can have a marriage or long-term relationship that works nicely. If two extremely short Lines perceive life as war, yet become partners fighting the world in the same bunker, they can create a strong bond and a strong partnership.

Longer Lines, who have never really experienced deep emotional traumas, survival, hatred and defensiveness, often try to pull Shortlines out of their bunkers to change them into Pollyanna types, rather than join them in the fight. That type of relationship can soon turn into a domestic civil war, as both believe the other's perception of life is crazy.

MATCH YOUR LINE

Do not lie to yourself about your love past or the characteristics of your own Relationship Capacity Line. Take an honest assessment of yourself.

The closer you get to finding a compatible Matchline, the less likely the problematic mismatch dynamics will be operative in the relationship. If you are not already in a committed relationship and seeking one, then your goal is to find a Match with a Line very much like yours (or as close to it as you can find), and stop these painful reactions from getting started.

If you are already in a committed relationship, then your challenge is to learn how to balance **differing Lines** successfully. If you are the Longline in the relationship, then the bulk of the work to achieve that balance will be up to you.

Both in an existing relationship and in a search for a new one, if you reach too high above your own Relationship Capacity Line, thinking that you can deny the truth about your own Shortline status in relation to them, you will become miserable and so will your mate. If you think you can lengthen a Shortline by exuberantly showing them how to love you better, you may force them to try to escape you. Chances are you may already have experienced this—maybe even more than once.

The good news is that **nearly all Relationship Capacity Line levels can make workable relationships.** The primary consideration for relationship success is the balancing of the Line Gap between your Line Ceiling and theirs.

If you are the Longline in your relationship, you may have already experienced the Line Gap of loneliness that soon becomes unfulfilled gut-ache, then starts the negative reactions, and eventually stresses the relationship. When the Line Gap is substantial, the relationship will be painful for both the Shortline and the Longline.

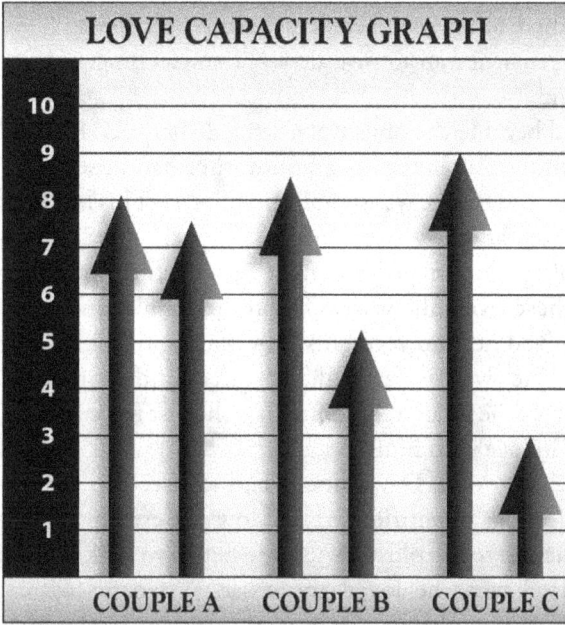

LOVE CAPACITY GRAPH

COUPLE A   COUPLE B   COUPLE C

If you are already in a committed relationship, then your challenge is to learn how to balance differing Lines successfully. If you are the Longline in the relationship, then the bulk of the work to achieve that balance will be up to you.

♥

DAVID'S CROSSROAD

David's Line began to shorten before he was born. His biological father died in an auto accident before ever seeing his son. His mother remarried an abusive alcoholic and let his grandmother care for David.

David became the object of a struggle between his mother and his grandmother, after his grandmother had raised him for five years. At thirteen, he was stepping in to protect his mother from his violent stepfather.

In college, he married a woman with nurturing family values of the highest level. She was a giver to her family and to her work. David loved her; however, his Line was significantly shorter and flawed. He was unfaithful, ashamed and unfaithful again. Sometimes she retaliated, sometimes she just felt crushed. Always, she felt in love with him.

At a crisis point, David finally had to select his family over his mixed feelings of entitlement and low self-esteem and learned to stop reacting to his old wounds. He began to look at his past and prioritized what he loved the most. When his wife saw him sincerely making changes she made the decision to give him another chance. Fortunately, for both of them, David managed to save the love of a good woman.

Part 2

LINE BALANCING

"Some of us think holding on makes us strong:
but sometimes it is letting go."

—Hermann Hesse

Chapter 6
BALANCING WITH A SHORTLINE

*H*ere is one of the counter-intuitive secrets of balancing the Line Gap between a Longline and a Shortline: A relationship with a Shortline requires the Longline to **withdraw** (remember the cat?). That is the complete opposite of what you would instinctively think is right! This needed distance of withdrawal becomes greater as the size of the Line Gap is greater. The greater the Line Gap, the more distance the Shortline needs.

LIVING WITH A SHORTLINE

When you are the Longline, you must withdraw your attempts at closeness to the extent that the Shortline feels comfortable. Perhaps this means you will do more activities alone, rely on your shorter Line spouse or partner for only necessary social engagements that they can tolerate and be happy with only sporadic intimacy. These sacrifices are far more tolerable when the Longline understands that the Shortline is maxed out and not withholding love. Isolation becomes intolerable for someone with a very long Line.

For the Longline, there is not less work in a relationship with a Shortline; there is only less reward in terms of attention and fun. A relationship with a Shortline requires more sacrifices and compromises by the Longline. Sadly, the benefits are significantly fewer for an extreme Longline whose relationship suffers from a severe Line Gap.

Eventually, if balance in the relationship cannot be achieved, Longlines may ultimately say to themselves, "This relationship is meeting so few of my needs that it may not be such a great deal for me!"

Is the Line Gap between you and your partner small enough to balance and thereby achieve a healthy degree of harmony?

STATIC ON THE LINE

If you are the Longline in the relationship, then understand that Longlines often seem to be **critical** of Shortlines, even if they never say a word or never behave aggressively. Longlines work so hard to improve Shortlines' love ability that very soon Shortlines can clearly see they are "shorter" by comparison and the result is they begin to **feel inadequate.** A Longlines' compassion, sympathy, assistance or nagging, all feels similar and patently insulting to the Shortline. Sweet affection backfires badly in the Longline's face.

"Obviously you think you are better than I am," thinks the Shortline subconsciously. "Well, I'll fix you."

When a Shortline finally perceives this discrepancy in the relationship with a Longline, he or she will naturally attempt to establish a semblance of equality—and since he or she can't go up, the only alternative left is to bring the Longline down to the Shortline's level.

Often, Shortlines tend to hurt the innocent Longlines by putting them down verbally, emotionally, and sometimes even physically. The shortest Lines may betray their Longline partners and emotionally incapacitate them in order to even the score in their minds. Moreover, they feel righteous in doing so, because they think the Longlines are acting superior and actually deserve a little "humbling."

This whole process happens in such subtle subconscious ways that most Shortlines would openly deny the existence of such behavior or motivation; however, the Longline *feels* it.

Unfortunately, if you are the Longline in the relationship, you translate bad feelings from the relationship into lower self-esteem and an *urgency to work harder* to make everything feel better. However, in doing so, you only do more of what triggers your partner's discomfort with you. This tactical error is what begins the cycle that spirals downwards. When this happens, the Shortline (whether just a bit short or a lot) is leaning away from a Longline, gasping for space while a Longline persists in leaning over into the face of the Shortline. This behavior is a big mistake—and guaranteed to pour ice-cold water on your partner's passion for you.

If your heart is broken, ask yourself, "Was I the Longline in this relationship?" Perhaps this is the agonizing answer to what went so wrong, what caused the breakup, the reason why your partner cruelly dumped you after you did so much, gave so much, or tried your hardest?

CROSSED LINES

> **Longline to Shortline:** *"How about going to the gym and working out with me. I know how much you love lifting weights. Afterwards, we can go for a walk on the beach."*
>
> **Shortline hears:** *"You are lazy, why don't you get off your couch and exercise?"*
>
> **Shortline says:** *"I cancelled my membership to the gym and I've joined a running club. Besides, I hate the beach. You go without me."*

ARE YOU CHEATING?

Can you guess who is going to have an affair and become the cheating partner? Will it be the desperate, starved for love Longline, the one who has been rejected and treated with indifference repeatedly? Not likely...

The Longline's self-esteem is at its lowest possible point, forcing him or her to question his or her own value and sexual attractiveness. Longlines stay home, eat more and become depressed.

The Shortlines are at the greatest risk of being unfaithful to their partners. While being prodded for more and more, and repeatedly reminded that they do not have enough to offer, Shortlines are very likely to seek out new, re-energizing relationships filled with refreshing feedback. Feedback such as "I don't know why your awful partner doesn't appreciate you! You are the best thing that ever happened to me," as stated with great sincerity and affection by the shortest Lines. The earnest Longline is quickly replaced by a cute, sweet-acting Shortline, who beneath his or her showy façade behaves like a dangerous relationship-carnivore.

A Longline can unwittingly push a Shortline into the eager arms of a new lover—someone who has much lower expectations and makes the Shortline partner feel like a winner instead of a chronic failure. You already know the ending: The Shortline dumps the loving Longline and buys the new lover a red sports car.

This cycle continues to replay itself until—and unless—harmony, balance and stability are reached. It is only a matter of time until the new couple's Lines either align or repel each other. If they are completely mismatched, the relationship is likely to be destined for the dustbin. However, if they are lucky enough to match up accidentally, the relationship can thrive. The now devastated self-esteem of the poor Longline increasingly lowers his or her chance for success in the relationship market.

CROSSED LINES

Longline says to Shortline: *"How could you miss little Tommy's swim meet? You are heartless."*

Bottomline says to Shortline: *"You poor thing. You work so hard. I don't know why she does not appreciate you, Honey. You meet my needs completely. You are the best thing that ever happened to me."*

Shortline hears: *"Bottomline thinks I'm great just the way I am, not like that Longline nag I live with. When can I move in with Bottomline?"*

Although the Longline is left abandoned and grieving, the Shortline will only look toward the relief and happiness of a new partner (for a while).

Longline sobs and asks, "What is missing in me? What did I do wrong?"

In reality, the Longlines' "problem" is that they have too much to give, not too little. Excess is what creates the Longlines' problems rather than a lack of loving ability.

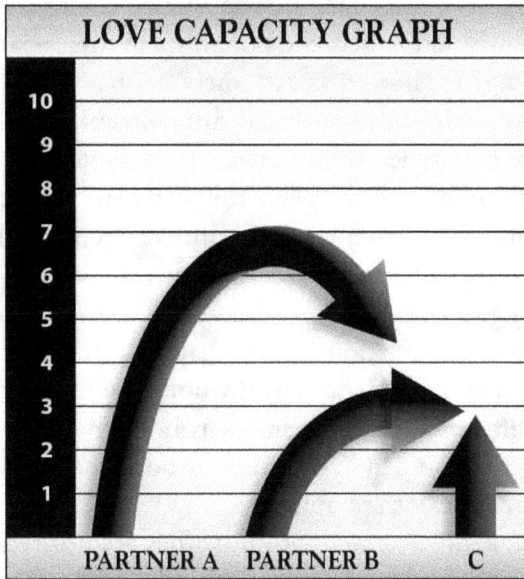

LOVE CAPACITY GRAPH

PARTNER A   PARTNER B   C

A Longline can unwittingly push a Shortline into the eager arms of a new lover—someone who has much lower expectations and makes the Shortline partner feel like a winner instead of a chronic failure.

Can They Change?

Some room for change is essential for an enduring relationship. Unfortunately, people with very short Lines, by definition, typically cannot reverse severe damage to their ability to trust, care deeply and give. If they do accept that there is a need for them to change, they must struggle to establish a new belief system, one in which love is wonderful and not supposed to hurt. Rather, their fears keep them locked up, more rigid in relationships and more afraid of anything new. They may not be able to change themselves even if they are highly motivated to become Longlines in their relationships.

Significant change for *anyone* is extremely hard and takes dedication and motivation. People who have endured difficult childhoods are often less flexible and more frightened. In essence, a person whose Line is very short may also be weaker in overall character strength from early childhood abuse. You certainly cannot make your partner improve or change. It is unlikely that people change just for their partners, although, everyone can change a lot for themselves if they choose to.

The reality of a loving relationship ultimately depends upon the behavior and cooperation of another person, over whom you have little or no control. Shortlines have difficulty understanding why Longlines give "excessively" and then want (demand) so much in return. It just does not compute.

This is frustrating for both people.

Longlines mistakenly assume that Shortlines are not really that different from themselves, and therefore must have hidden resources and capacities to love buried somewhere inside them and are holding back. Longlines reason that if they give enough love, as one might smother love a child, then untapped potential can surely be discovered in the Shortline. The Longline reasons that this potential can be brought out by giving more affection and attention.

Unfortunately, that is not how it works.

FILL IN THE GAPS

Shortlines resent the feeling that their freedom is being robbed when their Longline partners try to control them, ask too much of them or try to change them under the cloak of "improving" them to make them a better person.

If you are the Longline in your relationship and your Shortline partner makes you happy, then you can Line Balance to keep the relationship. You will need to accept and learn to deal with most of your Shortline's limitations. Remember, Shortlines have an ideal partner, too, and it is probably not you in many ways. Therefore, if you decide to keep your Shortline partner, then think seriously about changing your invasive behavior enough to let him or her breathe. You might fill in your Line Gap with other love objects in your life who would appreciate your attention and warmth: like elderly folks, young people, pets, projects or causes. By creating distance, you will "love" your partner the way he or she *needs* to be loved, and to your surprise, you may discover your partner will adore you for doing so—as much as they can.

CROSSED LINES

> **Longline to Shortline:** *"I love you so much, I've cooked a romantic dinner and hand-knitted you a sweater for your birthday with yarn I spun myself."*
>
> **Longline says to Self:** *"If I show him how I go all out for his birthday, maybe he'll finally buy me something special for mine."*
>
> **Shortline says to Self:** *"All this love and self-sacrifice from her is making me feel smothered and unworthy—again. I think I'll drink too much wine at dinner and then sleep on the couch."*

You cannot make your partner grow a longer Line. Usually, no one wants unsolicited help. Unsolicited help implies that you are competent and they are incompetent. Try cutting a Shortline's steak, selecting his or her clothes, or exhibiting other super-smothering behavior and watch him or her soon want to attack you back. The more Longlines adore and try to help, the more their partners are insulted and repulsed. Before understanding Matchlines dynamics, you may have been once shocked and surprised by their negative reaction to your beautiful onslaught of affection. Now you are beginning to see how Longlines demean their Shortline partners when they "correct and teach" them.

Furthermore, never ever love partners like children. If they ever get the notion that you are trying to be their parent, the passion is over. Any attempt to change a Shortline's patterns and beliefs must be the Shortline's idea and goal, not the Longline's project. You can commit to personal change that can lengthen your Line, but the work is internal and does not involve the will of others. Above all, understand that your mate's expectations and your expectations of relationship behavior have to jive.

Because a person with a shorter Line may be less sensitive and dulled by life's disappointments and hurts, he or she may also need bigger sensations than a Longline to feel anything. The shorter the Line, the more likely the sad symptoms show. Some couples may seek out professional help to balance their Line Gap and to be successful in love. Unfortunately, those with extremely short Lines, tend to drink more, abuse drugs more, and go through more partners just trying to feel love, happiness or fun—just to feel anything at all.

Sometimes after prolonged rejection, the Longline in a large Line Gap relationship is in so much pain that he or she finally withdraws and begins to shut down emotionally, too. Ironically, the emotional distance this creates balances the relationship and is **appealing** to the Shortline. At last, the Shortline begins to pursue the Longline, yet he or she may steadfastly refuse to change any of his or her own behaviors. Often, the Longline will reciprocate with adoration ten fold and drive the Shortline out the door once more.

LONGLINE CONTROL

Do you have a nice Shortline, who is not addicted or mentally deranged, and a partner that you decide you really want to keep? If you do, it will have to be with the acceptance of the fact that you cannot extend anyone's Line.

Many wonderful people have dedicated their lives and sacrificed their happiness to this thankless task. All have failed. Line extension will only happen when change comes from within, not from outside influences.

Sometimes a miracle happens. On rare occasions, a person who has a near-death experience such as a car accident, a heart attack or a true connection with spirituality, has a long-lasting, cathartic and sincere recovery from childhood emotional trauma. The shock of the event seems to override the early trauma and bitterness. In place of defensiveness and resentment, a near-death experience can cause one's heart to fill with gratitude just for being alive. This is an exception in clinical practice. Otherwise, even small changes take hard work.

LINE DANCE

Most superficial "change" lasts less than a year or two. Just as you begin to trust again, the bad habits reappear. However, a relationship is very much like a dance—if you change your behavior in the relationship, then the relationship itself will change in some way, even if your partner does not want to budge emotionally or psychologically. Results are not always predictable. If the status quo is too painful and unacceptable, then you can *force* a measure of change in the relationship (not the other person) by implementing *your own* behavior changes.

What are Longlines to do to foster change in the relationship?

First, straighten up your own Relationship Capacity Line! Are you in your partner's face? Are you driving him or her away? You can change yourself right now and begin to balance your relationship with Line Balancing techniques.

The good news is that Longlines are predominantly in control of the relationship. A Shortline can often only react to the Longline's behavior. Initially, they are reacting to a force-feeding of too much love. When Longlines straighten up and stop the emotional pressure, then Shortlines can breathe again, and often a great deal of tension abates. Longlines can drive love away by smothering Shortlines, or they can choose to seduce love closer by substituting other love objects and by stepping back to relieve the pressure on the Shortline. Must you ignore your partner? Take your cues from your partner. When you have retreated to his or her reduced comfort level, your partner will begin to pursue you with all the attention you have been aching to have. Remember? Like it was in the beginning of your romance.

Keep recalling the cat analogy!

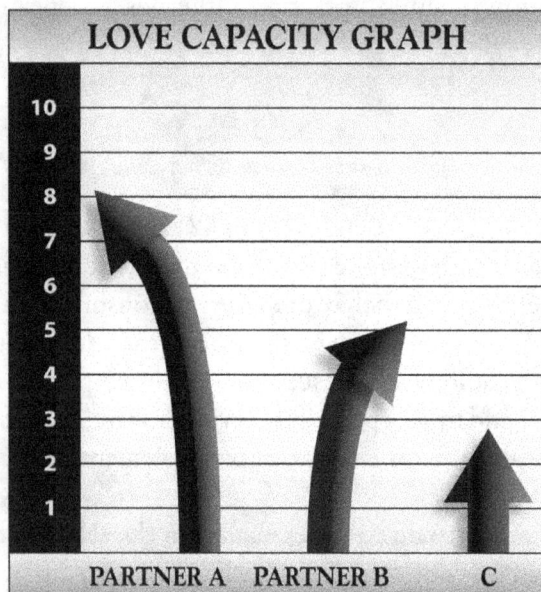

LOVE CAPACITY GRAPH

10 9 8 7 6 5 4 3 2 1

PARTNER A   PARTNER B   C

This achievement of balance, based on your partner's capacity to love rather than on your own, is the most important lesson in Matchlines. Giving space is a special form of loving a Shortline.

LOVE ME MY WAY

You can demonstrate love with total adoration and a thousand baby kisses, just as your mom and the movies taught you. Unfortunately, such excess attention will repulse the Shortline. Alternatively, you could sit quietly with a Shortline outside of his or her space peacefully. This is a form of loving your Shortline too, the right way!

CROSSED LINES

Shortline says to Longline: *"Sorry, I know we had plans, but I don't really feel like having dinner tonight. I might go over to Jerry's for awhile."*

Longline says to Shortline: *"That's fine. Some of my friends are going to a party tonight and I will go with them. There will be many new people there. I will try to have fun. I'll still miss you."*

Shortline says: *"Oh. Well, I guess I could probably eat some sushi at the party. I'll go with you."*

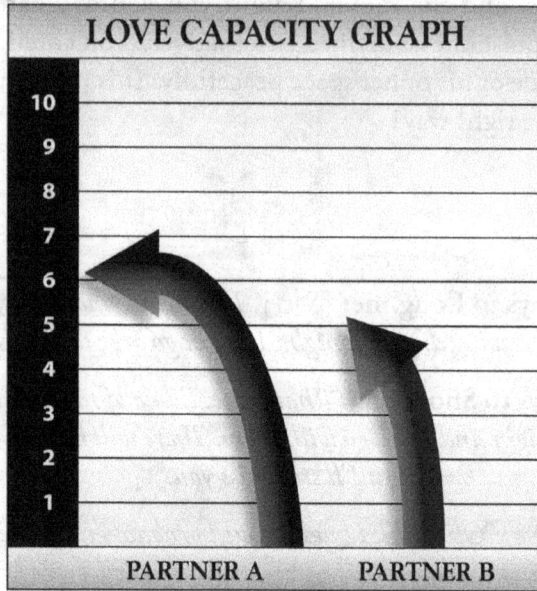

LOVE CAPACITY GRAPH

When you have retreated to his or her reduced comfort level, your partner will begin to pursue you with all the attention you have been aching to have.

❤

RAPE OR LOVE?

If you ignore your Shortline's signals to back off, then, effectively, you are being rude to your partner, not loving. If someone throws their arms around you and it gives you pleasure, then he or she is demonstrating love to you. However, if it makes you uncomfortable or you hate the closeness, then that very same act is not giving love. Instead, this is more rape-like, a violation, a taking of his or her fill, satisfying personal desires, at your expense. That is a form of abuse wearing affectionate clothing. So, likewise, do not let your needs dictate the amount of intimacy you give to a Shortline.

Have you come to realize that perhaps you have mistakenly been force-feeding love down your Shortline's throat? If so, then you also need to know that you may have done real damage to the relationship by now. Any positive move in your partner's direction will make him or her act like a rabid raccoon. You have to make your partner hungry for you. To do that, you must withdraw until he or she feels desire and wants to change direction to come toward you.

Obviously, this is not easy for you love-gluttons. Nevertheless, you have to withdraw until they are texting and calling you, bringing you flowers and searching the room for your eyes. You know what it feels like to have someone pursue you—to *want* you. You also know what it feels like when your partner is *not* looking at you, avoiding you and instead, checking out every other hot body in the room.

You must never make excuses for your partner's avoidance of you: "He's working too hard," "He's tired," or "I am too fat." We make up endless invalid excuses to rationalize a Shortline on the run.

Is it "loving" to sacrifice your intense needs for your partner's comfort? Yes, it is wonderful for him or her; however, it is not so great for you. Thankfully, Longlines are in more control of achieving balance in the relationship. Granted, this is an unconventional way to love someone, yet, it is just as valid and considerably more successful for a long-term relationship than many other methods.

Is it really unselfish and genuine love on your part to give only what you want, and only how you want to give it, rather than giving what your partner needs?

If you are the Longline in the relationship, then your next question for yourself is, "Can I bend far enough away from this relationship to achieve balance? And can I also significantly meet my own needs in such a way that my Shortline is able to feel comfortable and I don't starve?"

It is only when you distance yourself from your Shortline and create breathing room for him or her that he or she will stop rebelling from the relationship and begin to participate.

Recognize that if you are in a relationship with a Shortline, you need to back off. You are simply going to have to fulfill your smothering love needs somewhere else. Buy a dog, plant a garden, volunteer at a retirement home, or spend time with other Longline friends—the ones you have been ignoring while you smothered your partner.

Your behavior must bend your Line away—far away from your Shortline until your Shortline begins to feel at first comfortable, then a little hungry, then desirous of you. Even someone with a small appetite and a small stomach will eventually get hungry again.

At first, this experience will genuinely feel like torture and be impossible to bear for an attention-junkie love-glutton. If your desire is to give the relationship its best chance for success, then Matchlines Balancing can work for you.

However, you cannot just go on indefinitely without having your needs met, too. If Shortlines cannot give you more, where and when is a Longline finally fed? A Longline's needs must also be met. If you must bend so far away that you find yourself having almost *no interaction* with your Shortline, then talk to your therapist and perhaps seriously consider the possibility of seeking out a longer Line relationship, with someone new and more compatible—a better Matchline for you.

MOVE ON

Although initially painful, when the Line Gaps are irreparably large and emotionally damaging the Longline may decide that it is in his or her best interest to move on and find better matches with new, longer Lines. Longlines and Shortlines never have to stop having warm memories and loving feelings for their discarded beloveds. However, if you do find yourself in a severely toxic relationship, one that is clearly detrimental to your well-being, you must consider getting help to get away. A therapist can assist you with your escape from such a situation—as painlessly, amicably, and expeditiously as possible.

If the Line Gap is extraordinarily huge and the relationship has degenerated to "all out war" or extreme silent suffering all of the time (especially when severe emotional abuse or physical abuse is involved), seek out a good therapist who can help you to decide what is best for your family. Perhaps he or she will tell you there may be no other practical alternative for finding peace and happiness other than to terminate or at least, take a break from the relationship. Maybe separation is easier if you are only dating, but in deeply committed relationships, especially where children are involved, leaving is far more problematic. In most instances, an existing relationship deserves an opportunity to balance before you consider abandoning it, unless your partner is abusive to you, your children or your pets.

You have a right to be happy and peaceful even if that means starting over. Unfortunately, the longer the Line, the greater is the ability to sacrifice, persevere and endure. Longlines rarely walk out on someone for whom they feel compassion. They stay, suffer and try harder, thinking they can make it better with more effort and love.

Many people will voluntarily stay in a truly untenable relationship out of feelings of loyalty, obligation, their vows, religious values, fear of starting over and being alone and lonely again, or in deference to the constraints of their belief system. What they fail to realize is the cycle of pain they are voluntarily bringing upon themselves and their partner and their children.

Some relationships do not have longevity, no matter how hard either or both of you try. Try your best to make a relationship work, and never make a decision to terminate a committed relationship lightly or rashly. Just be willing to recognize a situation that is irreparable or dangerous. As great chess masters know, there comes a definitive point in any game when the outcome is certain defeat and that player gracefully resigns—not as an act of cowardice, but rather, a rational judgment of reality and act of respect for the other player's time. However, remaining friends with an Ex is commendable and is especially important when you share children, a work environment or friends.

"*You were made perfectly to be loved and surely I have loved you, in the idea of you, my whole life long.*"

—Elizabeth Barrett Browning

Chapter 7
BALANCING WITH A LONGLINE

So what do you do if you discover that you are the Shortline in a current relationship? If you are a Shortline living with a Longline, you have challenges of a Line Gap to deal with, too.

You can choose to improve your Line to help decrease the Line Gap with your partner. You will benefit by letting your Longline in on the secrets of Matchlines, as your partner will learn how to back off and let you breathe. It makes good sense to work toward saving an existing good relationship rather than gamble on a new relationship that may eventually struggle with the same issues. If you are not in a relationship right now, look back at past relationships and discover if Line discrepancies were at work prior to the breakup.

Two Shortlines can live in functional distance: "I give a little, and you give a little, and it works for us." It is possible for them to learn to understand each other, to have appropriate **expectations,** to give and take fairly, without all the criticizing. In that situation they are talking the same love language. Likewise, two matched Longlines often do very well together.

It is when the Line Gap is great that two people often emotionally torture each other unintentionally, and will continue to do so until they understand how to balance their Line Gap.

So if you are already in love with a Longline, then think about explaining

Matchlines theory to him or her. If you chose to, you can teach your "so willing" partner how to love you with less demonstrative intimacy so that you can feel comfortable and not smothered.

If you make a match with a Line that is too long for yours, you will be the one who feels stifled and smothered with too much love and sticky intimacy. Do not confuse a Longline's neediness with a dysfunctional partner's verbal abuse. The Longline is **kind** and needy. As the Longline begs for more attention, you feel like less of a winner and more like a failure.

Your best is just not good enough, and that hurts your feelings. A Longline's excessive and unfulfilled needs make you look bad all day, every day. You feel like you will never meet your partner's expectations, and he or she will begin to nag you in subtle, little ways. You might begin to make excuses to get away from your "better half." Does the Longline love seem demanding, obligatory and eventually, repulsive to you? You might even experience debilitating feelings of inadequacy, guilt or failure that makes you avoid the now miserable, whiny Longline.

If this describes you, realize that you are very vulnerable in this relationship situation, and may one day (if not already) find yourself in the arms of a much shorter Line—one who thinks you are great just as you are.

After all that criticism, such flattery and affirmation from a slick, very short Line just might sound like music to your ears. Suddenly, you are the Longline in your relationship. At last, you think you have found the secret—since you cannot raise your ceiling, then becoming a Longline is just a matter of finding someone with a Line that is shorter than yours is! However, you are asking for trouble if you mix with a dysfunctional partner.

Of course, the downside is that your original Longline lover is appalled that you prefer a "short" new partner to a Longline. Desperate and confused, the rejected Longline can turn into a hostile clinging mess and then proceed to complain repulsively even more. Therefore, can anyone blame you for spending a little pleasant quality time with the undemanding Shortline instead of enduring unrelenting criticism? In fact, the "loving" Longline in your life has effectively guaranteed that you will want to dump him or her, and (at least temporarily) choose the Shortline who does not seem to need anyone.

WHO IS WRONG?

Here is the shocking reality: Shortlines are simply reacting and behaving
Line appropriately. That is not to condone rejection, abandonment or
infidelity, rather to recognize that this is the natural path of least resistance of
these forces. If you happen to be the Shortline in your relationship, you may
not be interested in maximum intimacy, nevertheless you have a million other
great qualities that make you a fine Match and worth keeping. Just remember
your partner may be hungry and in pain that you do not understand.

Moreover, if you are the Shortline, then you will benefit greatly by sitting
down and patiently sharing this information with your Longline partner. Even
if you are the instigator of utilizing the theory of Matchlines, Longlines must
ultimately lead in this dance. Just as you might teach your partner in ballroom
dancing to lead you around the floor, you must teach your Longline the
Matchlines theory. Your partner must understand that to "back off" is the
most effective way to love you. Only then, can you stop rebelling from your
partner and start loving him or her in return.

Revealing your inner self, stripped of any protective defenses, is perhaps the
hardest thing you will ever do in life. Nevertheless, you deserve to be honest
with yourself and your partner about your limitations. If you can muster the
courage to do this, you will be pleasantly surprised to discover there is so much
relief when you stop faking and just get emotionally naked.

LAURA AND RICO

The following relationship case study illustrates the difficulties a Shortline
patient experienced.

> Laura had waited all her life for Rico. Rico was a longer Line than
> Laura was and he did not hesitate to offer Laura an engagement
> ring. Laura had everything in Rico that she had ever wanted in a
> man. She would have been happy, except that one thing troubled
> her. Rico's first wife had left him. Rico had tried everything to save

their marriage to no avail. Laura began to obsess jealously over visions of the ex-wife and Rico together, laughing, sharing and making love. The thought that Rico had been happier with the ex-wife was tormenting her. Rico assured Laura that his old relationship was in the distant past and that he loved only her. Yet, Laura could not let it go. She thought about it all the time and was considering leaving Rico when she came to therapy.

"Why am I ruining the best relationship that ever happened to me?" she asked.

After analyzing their love heritages, it was clear that Laura was a Shortline and Rico was smothering her. A high level of intimacy and commitment troubled her, and so she latched onto an imagined flaw, one that Rico could never change. No one can change the past or the experience of love relationships. A new lover has no right to punish you for the past. Laura was pushing Rico away, so that she could feel comfortable. She was doing this subconsciously without malice toward her lover. She cried deeply at her session, feeling guilty and helpless.

However, once she understood the principles of Matchlines, she was able to calm Rico's fears about losing her. She encouraged him to find other interests. This relieved the intensity and frequency of intimate moments and love gestures coming at her.

Rico was delighted because he finally knew how to make her happy. They felt confident that they could find a balance in their relationship.

Rico came to understand that Laura's rejection of some of his intimacy was necessary to enable her to stay in the relationship. Once Rico could re-frame and accept Laura's need for space, he could understand that she was not rejecting him personally. This is precisely the way she needed to be loved.

By relating to her with reduced intensity, Rico found a new and different way of loving Laura. Laura could openly accept a whisper rather than a shout of intimacy.

Rico donated time to the YMCA kid's basketball program as a referee, and became a beloved coach for eight-year-old kids. Rico needed to give a great deal, but Laura could not withstand all that he had to give. Laura and Rico's interactions became more positive and comfortable and eventually reduced the tension between them.

An understanding of Matchlines (and recognizing the differences in the way your partner needs to be loved from how you want to love them) can be the key to keeping a good relationship from falling apart.

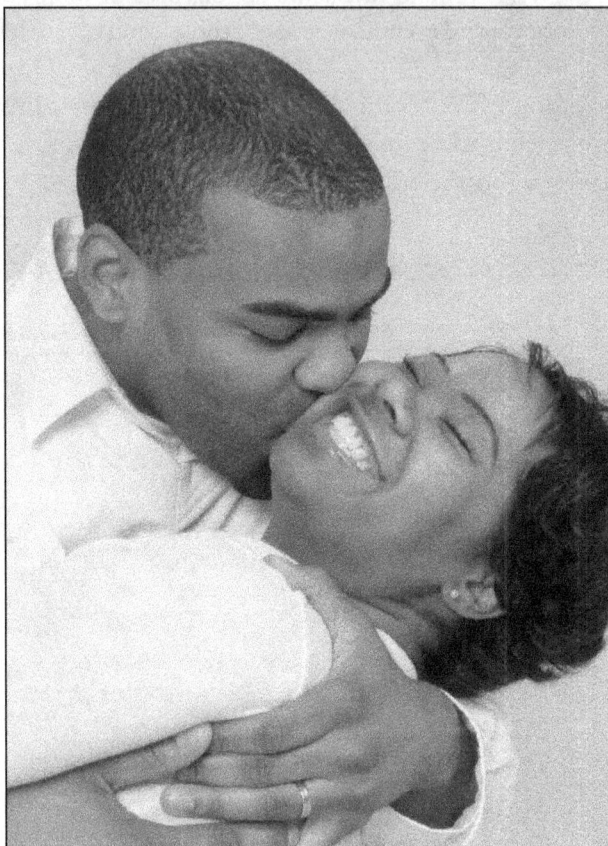

> "There are three things that last: faith, hope
> and love, and the greatest of these is love."

—Bible, I Corinthians 13:13

♥

Chapter 8
INVESTMENT LINE BALANCING

*A*re you vacillating about breaking up or committing all the way with a new love? Try to imagine your relationship in money investment terms, and then perhaps your options will become crystal-clear. Think of your love relationship as an investment of your time, your money and a better part of your life with other people. At risk in your relationship are costly losses in terms of your mental health, your future children's happiness or years of grief for everyone.

Think of the person with whom you are having a relationship as a stock in which you are investing. Some stocks have big payoffs with tall spikes and subsequent lows with costly losses. Rarely, a spike may pay a thrilling fortune. Other stocks are steady yet yield low returns. The spiking stocks may appear better investments initially, until they drop out from underneath you. Then you find yourself paying back losses with your savings—heartbreak.

"Spikers" are not good investments. Even though you have intense body rushes and thrilling times, Spikers are not stable and they will crash, guaranteed. As in all gambling situations, you can become addicted to the highs and lows of the game. Addicted people are always less powerful people.

If you are lonely and depressed, you may think you need a big spike to spark up your life, like a quick affair that you know is doomed. You learn from experience that impulsive quick fixes to your emotional pain are futile and addictive.

After the big spike, there typically comes the big fall that leaves the longer Line devastated. Big grief and prolonged recovery come hand in hand with that fall. Be aware that sometimes one, two or more years will pass as you recover from a relationship with a Spiker.

GOOD INVESTMENTS

As you grow older, you will find that a consistent payoff and dependability factor is more important than any high short-term spike. You may fantasize about wild, romantic love all you wish. However, a wise person outgrows a willingness to allow their heart to be trod upon for a quick spike and even quicker heartbreak.

Some Shortline stock does deserve consideration if it is dependable. Nevertheless, they might remain a bit too small for you. The Shortlines often perceive themselves as a blue chip stock because they are giving their best love to you. Their 100% effort results in a meager return based on their Line ability. They may be really stretching to give you what you are already getting from them. Unfortunately, their love feels more like a penny stock than a blue chip stock to you.

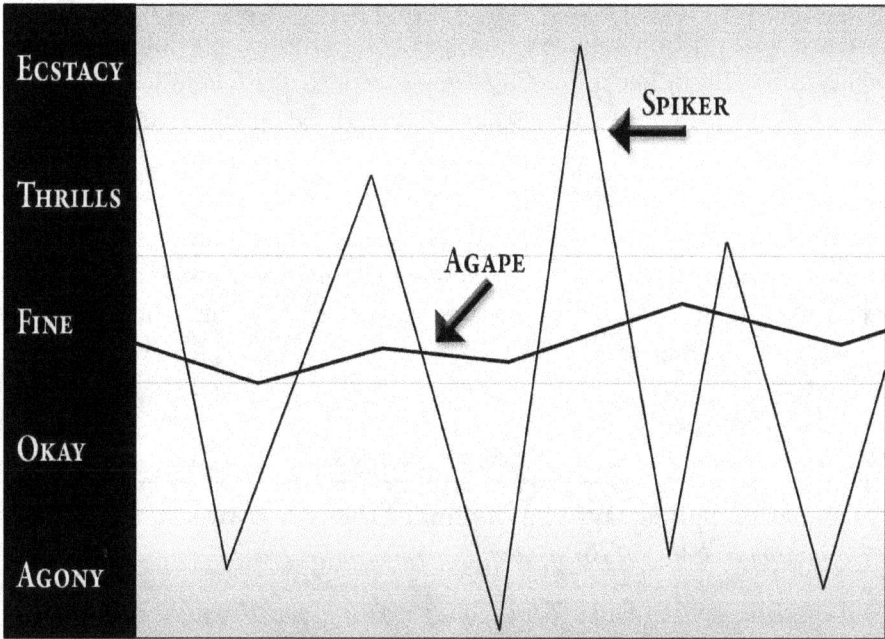

"Agape Love" is defined as a steady, dependable love without drama or conditions.

BREAKING UP IS HARD TO DO

In the beginning of a relationship, you see all of a person's good points. During a break up, you see only the bad. You may have felt a lovely, golden warmth toward you partner at first. You thought he or she was It, and then the romance wore off. You still see yourself as a blue chip stock, while your partner begins to lose his or her shine. Once you accept that this is your partner's best offering in the love department, then you can decide if what you are receiving is only worth a penny to you, or much more. For some other person, your partner might be a perfect Match, a blue chip winner. It is not about your partner's inadequacies as much as it is about the relationship itself being wrong—a bad Match. The two of you are simply not a good fit. There is no need to find faults or to blame. Perhaps you decide that it is time to let it go.

CROSSED LINES

Shortline Spiker says to Longline: *"There's a great new club open downtown. Let's go! Bring your cute roommate, too."*

Longline says to Self: *"I love doing exciting new things like this with him. I am not sure if he really likes me or is he after my roommate?"*

Longline Agape says to Longline: *"Hey, I was at the grocery store and they had that protein drink I know you like, so I bought you some. I got your mom some too."*

Longline says to Self: *"Protein drinks aren't real exciting, but he sure is considerate."*

Do not try to alter your partner. It does not work. People usually revert to who they are and want to be. Just like a raging river under pressure, the well-traveled habits easily follow the original course in spite of bridges, dams, threats, loss, extensive counseling or good intentions. If you attempt to change your partner into acting like a blue chip stock for you, the ultimate feeling that you will project to him or her is "Gee, you're not living up to my expectations; you're not behaving like a blue chip stock. You just keep coming in at a penny. You're here; however, you're just not enough for me."

If you are disappointed, your partner will perceive that disappointment loud and clear. That makes him or her feel like a failure, and it ends the romance.

So what can you do if you find out that you are involved with a good penny stock partner? Assuming that you perceive yourself as a blue chip stock, there are big dollar differences to consider, otherwise known as the Line Gap.

Should you take those dollar differences and foolishly give that to your partner? Do you stuff your partner with your excessive love? No! If you do, then you are going to feel ripped off and your partner is going to be overwhelmed.

FORGET MINE, FORGET YOURS

If you remember your mate's birthday, but he or she forgets yours, you are putting blue chips worth of effort into this relationship and you come up short big bucks. Your stomach will feel bad, you will begin to obsess and get depressed, and you may eat vast amounts of ice cream to feel better, but that will not help you. You will turn into a resentful sulker and even this penny investment is going to dump you. You have successfully become a Skyline smothering a Shortline!

However, let us consider this. Why throw away a consistently paying penny stock? That is not good business. Could you keep the penny stock and reframe your expectations? Assuming that you are not already in a deeply committed relationship with your partner, perhaps you can try changing the way that you are looking at this investment.

DIVERSITY

Would you sell a good stock that was paying a steady return for the hope that you may find another stock that might pay more? That is not smart. Do you throw every relationship away in order to seek a mysterious, elusive, blue chip stock that somewhere in your imagination might be just around the next corner? No way! There might be a long drought with no relief.

Okay, first try to keep your penny investment, but "take back" any excess that you are investing. Step back and give your partner the same kind of relationship your partner is giving to you. That does not mean to act mean or cruel or try hard to be negative or distant. Just do not pursue or push your partner. Just enjoy what he or she can give to you. If your partner is a big drinker, only go to lunch with him or her. If your partner refuses to dance, try going bowling with him or her instead. Turn your relationship into a winning penny experience. However, factor in nights that you go out to dinner with someone else who is sober. Go play golf or buy dance lessons. If you are in a committed relationship, then you do activities with friends, not with people you are sexually attracted to, or people who threaten your partner. You must end the restrictions of your life just because of your partner's limitations. Effectively, this is someone you are just "dating as a friend," not your dream mate.

Tremendously reduce the effort that you are putting into the relationship. If they are good at being your ten percent partner, enjoy that ten per cent. If you are starving, you do not throw back a crust of bread because it is not a sandwich. It is possible that this person is not, nor will ever be, your true love. Perhaps you will choose not to give the pleasure of your body, your fidelity, or ever prioritize this person over your kids or parents. This partner may choose to move on. If a partner wants you to give much more to him or her than he or she can give back to you, that is not a good deal for you. If you have tried hard to make it work, maybe let them ride off into the sunset—alone.

JENNY PAYS HALF

Jenny was the perfect, hardworking mate. Rather than risk making waves, she allowed her husband to take advantage of her. She was falling out of love, and she did not want that to happen. With a little help, Jenny expanded her world so that her man would be enough.

Jenny was married to John, an accountant who was cheap. He was nice, slovenly, overweight and lazy. Jenny worked hard on the house, the dogs, the cars, the relationship, the relatives, and remembered all birthdays and anniversaries. Jenny's list of efforts was Herculean.

John had announced that when they married they should share expenses. Jenny passively agreed to anything anyone wanted, and so she agreed with John. In fact, she was proud of paying her half, because she felt it provided her a voice and some power in the relationship.

They had been married for about ten years when Jenny came to therapy. John's income had increased every year of their marriage. He had two personal secretaries, plus Jenny at home. Jenny also worked in the hospital, caring for intensive care patients. She worked hard for her money. She came home tired to clean the house and to make dinner. He stayed at his important office work until she called him home for dinner. He did the dishes after dinner, and then fell asleep on the couch in front of the television.

Because he had such a large income, he decided when and where they would vacation, or if they would eat out. Jenny accepted this because he paid for so much.

Jenny was fooling herself.

John's "half" of the expenses amounted to less than 20% of his salary. Jenny's share of the expenses was more than 80% of her take-home pay. She had no perks. No one brought her coffee or made a dentist appointment for her. She could never join her husband in his occasional afternoon golf game. The quality of her life in no way resembled the quality of her husband's. Understandably, she was depressed, resentful and miserable.

Valentine's Day was coming up. Every holiday Jenny did the works—buying carefully selected expensive presents, fancy gift-wrapping and three or four cards. He usually gave her a gift certificate from a department store and a joke card. This time I suggested that she get him one card and one small gift. She was to hide the gift until after he gave her a present. She was doubtful, yet complied with my instructions.

John said he had forgotten about Valentines Day and had to work late so he only had time to get her a card. She handed him his card, a joking one, and said lightly, "Oh that's fine. I didn't get you anything either." She saw his jaw clench and his pudgy brow wrinkle. He hardly talked that night and the next day a dozen roses and a "smoochy" card arrived at her nurse's station.

Jenny knew then that she was on the right track. She then began to focus her day around achieving her life goals rather than his. She has since finished a master's degree and increased her income. She hired a cleaning service and insisted that he pay the majority of the fee. They split the bills with a percent of each salary instead of all of hers and a little bit of his. Now she is in charge in her life just as he is in charge in his life.

Balance achieved.

EXPAND YOUR PORTFOLIO

"Expanding your love portfolio," means that you just let the current relationship find its own level. Let it be a penny relationship if it is. That leaves you a lot of time and effort to invest somewhere else. You must be open to finding more stocks if what you already have does not meet your current portfolio needs. You need to keep shopping, buying and selling until you get a nice return on the money/effort that you have to invest.

Somewhere out there is at least a solid dependable stock that is capable of meeting most of your needs. If you just keep paying and losing, then you have to keep moving. You cannot make your ultimate goal just to marry someone, because that goal will cloud the idea of finding a good match. It may be necessary to diversify in order to meet your needs.

You cannot give all of yourself in a mismatch. If you are not married or in a committed relationship, and fidelity is one of the qualities that your penny stock is giving to you, that is going to make you feel guilty for trying to fill your deficit.

When they say, "But I love you, and I want you to be true to me," you could say, "I have needs that you cannot meet. I care for you, and I want to continue our relationship. However, you do not fulfill all my needs even though you say that I fulfill all of your needs. I do not want to settle for less than what I want in a relationship while still doing all the work."

You must be completely honest with your current partner. If you are married, tell your partner that you are going to do more activities with friends. If you are single, tell them that you are dating others and looking for new stocks. Tell them that they are free to continue a partial relationship with you, to lose their compressors, get therapy or to break it off completely. If you choose to trade your exclusivity for one penny's worth of relationship, then you should leave the trading floor!

You are selling yourself short.

OUT OF STOCK

If you are in a situation where you are working on a career, or you are taking care of children or aging parents, do not kid yourself that you are available to perform like a blue chip stock, you are not. You may be desperately lonely for a relationship, but you are not "available" to give enough for a successful love relationship. You will make excuses for your dilution of attention: it is my job, my kids, my parents or my depression. Nevertheless, you cannot give a relationship the time and energy it requires.

The abandonment or disloyalty of your partner is a stinging blow when you are already down and overburdened. Can you expect him or her to sacrifice his or her needs because you want to be head of the PTO, a star, a perfect parent or a doctor? Only Skylines can run on empty. If you do not have much left over to offer a partner, be aware that this might put him or her in a situation where he or she needs to diversify from you.

Sometimes just "being married" seems more important than finding true love, or a Matchline. A person who is not married or pursued is often ridiculed and perceived as less valuable in our society. Some people would marry anyone who held still long enough for them to slip a ring on their finger. Some people would choose to stay in a bad marriage rather than face the horror of being "unmarried." In some cultural environments, if people are not married off by a certain age, society considers them less in some way. Think about all the times a friend you have not seen in a while starts a conversation off with the question, "So are you still single?"

The misery of settling for a committed relationship where you are putting in a blue chip effort and getting a penny return is simply not worth it. The disappointment, boredom and unfulfilled needs eat away at you while you pretend to have a Norman Rockwell picture of laughing children and a happy spouse. No one else can see your fantasy. However, they may see your sad eyes.

DREAM MAKERS

Go ahead and benefit from your penny stock, while you keep your head together. Try to avoid looking at this penny stock and saying, "If I just love him or her enough he or she will turn into the blue chip partner of my dreams."

If you find yourself making excuses for your partner, "The reason she drinks is because I upset her." Or, "Oh, he had a hard childhood and so he can't be nice to me now"—any excuses at all, means you are likely lying to yourself.

Consider reducing your involvement and your expectations to a point where you feel like you are both giving equally. Even though you may want to give more to the relationship, "more" will not make the stock improve on its payoff, nor does it increase your dividends. In reality, it will only cost you more for the little bit you get back from him or her. You will eventually feel broke.

One of the most important principles behind Matchlines is that no matter how much you invest, you are not going to change the returns on your partner's stock substantially, if at all. You are buying exactly what is there, no more, no less. Think twice about throwing away hard-earned money on imaginary potential. Look for a proven track record and find solid evidence of good past and current relationships before you come to any conclusions.

If your partner is not on speaking terms with his or her ex-spouse, eldest son or daughter, or mother, then watch out. If you buy the hype of, "We will just work out these problems over time," or, "If I just love him or her enough, it will all be fine," you may be fooling yourself, throwing away your time, your money and your life. A good Matchline is worth the wait.

CROSSED LINES

> **Bottomline says to Longline:** *"As soon as I write my screenplay, we are going to be rolling in dough, babe."*
>
> **Longline says to Bottomline:** *"I believe in your talent. It's just that you're not making any money, and so far, all you've written are a few paragraphs for your script."*
>
> **Bottomline says to Longline:** *"Well, if the house weren't such a mess and the dogs barking, I might be able to get more done."*

YOU ARE THE APPRAISER

What if a "penny stock" argues with you that he or she is really a blue chip stock? Your partner tells you, "Look I am a blue chip stock, and the real problem is that you are only investing a penny. You are not appreciating me!"

That is your partner's opinion. However, you know you best. A penny stock is someone with a short Line who cannot possibly know what is best for a Longline. You are the only one who knows the worth of this relationship to you. Nobody else can tell you what the value of this relationship is to you— not your friends, your mother, your kids, and certainly not your partner.

If it feels like you are putting in more to this relationship than what you are getting out, and your partner is telling you it is still not enough, then seriously consider letting the relationship go rather than beating yourself up with this kind of conflict. Ask a neutral therapist what he or she thinks before you act.

A Shortline's perception of what value he or she has to give to the relationship is based on the limits or "ceiling" of his or her own Line. The shorter the Line, the more distorted his or her sense of self-worth becomes. Is there a huge difference in what your partner calls a blue chip stock and what you call a blue chip stock?

Big differences in Lines rarely, if ever, close.

Fill Up

If you are someone with a long Line, and you choose to keep a quality Shortline, then it is time to fill the empty space of the Line Gap so you can change starving and sacrificing expressions to a happy smile.

Now that you know how to make your relationship more balanced by leaning away, not towards your Shortline, seriously consider taking your extra energy, love or money and spending it on yourself. Go to college one night a week instead of serving your partner's "poker game friends" their beer and chips. If your partner wants to hang out at the bar, then go to see your kind of movie. If you spend every weekend on the soccer field, take one weekend to visit museums with the kids.

Every time you do something fun for yourself, you get stronger and more independent—*emotionally* filled-up instead of starving. Meeting some of your own needs is the most powerful act a Longline can do to bring you healthier, saner relationships.

Concentrate on building up your Line, not changing someone else's. When you are thriving, you will attract a different brand of new partner than when you are in a miserable state. If you are already in a committed relationship, your old partner will start to react to you in a new, good way with Matchline Balancing.

Quality partners meet the majority of your needs. Finding most of the positive qualities you need in a partner can be sufficient when you have your own base of high self-esteem and joi de vivre. If you are still looking, when a true Matchline comes into your life—and he or she will come—the reward of a healthy, loving, stable relationship is worth the wait.

Part 3

LINE TYPES

"*My bounty is as boundless as the sea, my love as deep. The more I give thee, the more I have, for both are infinite.*"

—William Shakespeare

Chapter 9
SKYLINES AND BOTTOMLINES

Skylines are the longest Lines and great big givers. They will give you anything that they can. The rarely found Skylines give unselfishly, unconditionally, and generously with no catch and no expected payoff. Skylines are usually defenseless, vulnerable and innocent, sometimes naïve, and get deeply hurt often. Nothing in their lives prepares Skylines for the deceptive and desperately cruel world of Bottomlines.

Bottomlines are the opposite of a Skyline and cruelly reject the Skyline gifts of love. Yet, continual rejection does not stop Skylines from seeking out every needy-looking character they can find until they end up adopting a Bottomline as a project. These eternally optimistic souls think they can make a Bottomline's deficits "all better." There is only one direction in such a mismatched pair and it is down, down, down—never up.

Soon, abused Skylines begin to reject themselves, too. Continually rejected by shorter and shorter Lines, especially people like selfish Bottomlines, Skylines start to believe that they must be unlovable.

The truth is just the opposite.

Most people do not have the capacity to love a Skyline or handle the roar of love they are capable of delivering. If you are a Skyline, you are probably saying in despair, "That's just great, I still end up alone." However, that does not have to happen—if you play it smart. To do so, you must discipline yourself to avoid Bottomlines completely and back far away from any severely mismatched relationship.

CROSSED LINES

Bottomline says to Skyline (at 2 a.m.): *"My car broke down, I'm three hours away and I've got no cash. Could you pick me up and drive me to my friend's house?"*

Skyline to Self: *"Wow, she/he really needs me. That makes me so happy! I'll still be on time for my presentation tomorrow morning, if I hurry."*

The Line of a Skyline is so long that almost everyone in his or her life is a rejecting Shortline in comparison. If you do not use Matchlines Balancing, then you could eventually experience an increasing stream of abuse from your Shortline partner. Such abuse intentionally drives you back, away from personal space, like a growling dog issuing a warning, or a rattlesnake shaking his rattle. As you continue to intrude on the satiated Shortline, you are poking the rattlesnake. Even nice people will strike out at you to make you stop pushing and intruding.

This means that if you are the Longline in the relationship, or a Skyline, then sometimes people can hurt you, cruelly, painfully, viciously because you do not **hear** them. Nevertheless, undaunted and so forgiving, you mistakenly try harder and harder, as though sheer effort will one day make your partner slap his forehead in awestruck realization as though awakened from a coma and say, "Oh, now I see! I love you. What a fool I've been."

Although you may endlessly long for love and intimacy, you can never adequately fulfill and satisfy your own needs from a maxed-out Shortline. They simply do not have enough of what you want. Consequently, unless you change your actions, you can count on being disappointed, most likely pushed away and left alone.

NICE SKYLINE

Sadly, Skylines are often mistreated, abandoned, and are very confused because, in general, they are genuinely nice, loving people. Their big, soft hearts love anyone and anything that allows them to smother-love, yet somehow they rarely match up with another Skyline, who is the one they really need.

As an extreme Longline, a Skyline is giddy on life and feels everything from rapture to despair. They do not need two stiff drinks before they get up and dance. Life bubbles out of them; they laugh easily and love to be close and intimate. That is, until they are repeatedly devastated by hurtful relationships.

If you happen to be a Skyline living with a demoralizing Bottomline, try to recall who you were as a child, back when you really liked yourself, before you became interested in love relationships. If you are a Skyline, then you must realize that "smothering" is not "**loving**." Yes, you have good intentions. However, your good intentions are giving you terrible results.

If you had wonderful, adoring, affectionate parents and relatives, you are probably trying to love your partner that exact same way as love was modeled and taught to you. Unfortunately, it is too much for most of the population to handle.

As cynical as it might sound, the truth is, most people out there have been hurt and beat-up by life—a lot. Gushy, mushy, smothering, intense overtures of love and affection is the province of fiction, puppies and toddlers, not most adult lovers—especially not distant Shortlines. They will run from your sweet, gushing love as surely as if you were trying to inflict them with physical pain. However, you, right now, are in a perfect position to change this picture by engaging in Matchlines Balancing techniques.

BOTTOMLINES

In search of satisfying and gratifying love, Longlines reach all the way down into the bottom of the barrel looking for anyone to accept them. Enter the **dysfunctional personality** who may feign attraction temporarily, called a **Bottomline**. Bottomlines are severely damaged personalities and are big takers who are often charming and seductive. Mistaking initial attraction and flirtation as genuine feelings of love, desperate Longlines strangle every last drop of affection and attention out of the initial interest from Bottomlines. The Bottomline often responds by cruelly striking back at the smothering attention, often violently. Such matches explain why nice people sometimes end up in sick, abusive relationships. Discarded again, the Longlines naturally blame themselves because they are so good at accepting responsibility.

CROSSED LINES

> **Bottomline says to Longline:** *"I am way too stressed out by your constant demands. All you do is criticize me. I'm going to the bar!"*
>
> **Bottomline means:** *"I feel inadequate and I'm going to go get drunk to forget my pain. I may meet someone new who likes me just the way I am."*
>
> **Longline thinks:** *"Wow. He is having a really bad day. I will be the designated driver so he can relax. At least that way, we get to spend some more time together."*

There are people out there with shorter Lines relative to yours, who are the shortest of all, to the point of having a non-functional Line. Everyone is a Longline compared with a true Bottomline. Bottomlines are not just people with a shorter Line. They are the extreme and often dysfunctional people who, even when they try with good intentions to act lovingly, end up selfishly hurting someone. Dysfunctional Bottomlines, at the very bottom of the chart, are capable of breaking your heart with little or no remorse.

They will be delighted to use you, and cruelly do it repeatedly, until they decide to leave you. While you vainly attempt to bring them up, they often struggle to put you down, successfully. A good Shortline is worth trying to balance and make adjustments to find a comfort level. A Bottomline is just too risky.

Bottomlines are not technically suffering from any mental illness. They have a pronounced lack of the ability to give or have empathy, resulting in lowered morality and a weaker character. They are just incredibly self-centered and thoroughly content to stay that way. Most often, they have been neglected children who learned to trust only their own company and rejected their need for intimacy.

Bottomlines do not need a relationship. They use a relationship. They may want fans to adore them, but are capable of breaking up with a partner right before a holiday to avoid buying a gift. They often have multiple partners at the same time. They do not experience any sense of moral guilt for their heartbreaking ways. They do not realize how unfair they are. They get away with it because, typically, they possess one or more of a few great attributes such as heart-jolting physical beauty, a Greek God physique, athletic ability, a performing arts talent, wit or ridiculously rich parents.

Bottomlines have only personal, self-serving interests, not concepts of love or true spirituality. They are utterly selfish people who only take. They focus entirely on themselves and on what you can do for them. They are not obligated to act nice unless they are working you, planning to steal your money, your body or your dignity. After all, in their view, they are entitled. They only care about their toys and temporal pleasures. They spend their days on hobbies and personal interests, at the gym, out on the boat, or washing their car, all to enhance their outer selves and power to possess you.

HOT, HOT, HOT

Bottomlines are often the most sexually attractive people you will ever encounter. They have the glamour, the excitement and mystique that Longlines never seem to have. Often, they drive the best cars, dress great, are lean, hard-bodied, and beautiful. They attract everyone because they play it cool. They act distant, hard-to-get and catlike. They have many dates, marry if it benefits them and divorce often. They seem always to land on their feet and quickly move on. They do not change, and they like themselves just as they are. Unfortunately, their disposable ex-partners are in therapy for years trying to decipher what went wrong: "We were so good together in the beginning!"

Bottomlines strike while a person is down and vulnerable, like a shark sensing a fish in distress—like after a divorce or break-up. They typically abandon you when you are no longer of any use to them. They make effective salespersons, even though they may rob their company when the boss is not looking. They have weak staying power and often bend away under pressure when you need them. Increasingly abusive, they make your burdens heavier, not lighter.

A relationship with a Bottomline can be especially bad for your self-esteem. You may become depressed, self-destructive and so miserable that you eat, drink or drug to excess, insuring that no one will want to go out with you, except maybe other Bottomlines.

Longlines must bend so far away from Bottomlines to achieve such a short Line's comfort zone that they end up in left field with none of their needs met. Unless a Longline has a weird desire to possess a high-maintenance, beautiful trophy, then the Bottomline-relationship is a lot of work for a minimal return.

Often Longlines will behave even nicer and more giving, hoping to elicit niceness from the Bottomline. You can model functional behavior twenty-four-seven, and Bottomlines will still kick you emotionally and delight in their control of the "great" you. It is a complete waste of your time.

To create balance with a Bottomline by extremely withdrawing, you will quickly starve for affection. Finally, you ask yourself, "What is the point of this relationship?" Sometimes a hysterical break-up follows, or sometimes you just quietly disappear and lick your wounds.

Eventually, you will have estranged, suppressed or killed off all your feelings until you finally begin to heal and start to get over them. Soon, you are numb and mercifully relieved from the heartache because you stop wanting him or her.

Time passes with no word. You could be dead for all he or she cares. Then suddenly the Bottomline is back! Your lack of emotion and distance makes you irresistibly attractive to the Bottomline. Now you appear to be a good fit because you demand nothing and expect nothing, and that is just what is needed and wanted! The Bottomline will pursue you and desire you. You think, at last, he or she has finally realized your true value and you are back on cloud nine. Watch out, the moment you become close and comfortable bending toward a Bottomline, he or she will start acting nasty.

Word to the Wise: Run fast before a Bottomline catches you and seduces you once again. You could spend a lifetime replaying the same scene, because the rejection-relief pattern is pure addiction, like the high and low of a drug.

CROSSED LINES

> **Bottomline to Longline:** *"I love you. Let's take a drive cross-country in my new Corvette to see my buddy, Jack."*
>
> **Longline to Self:** *"I can't believe somebody this good looking is going out with me—and we're going to travel together!"*
>
> **Bottomline to Longline:** *"Hey, Babe, I'm short on cash, so you'll have to pick up the tab. Sound fun, huh?"*

Although most people are attracted to a Bottomline like a moth to a flame, the Bottomline is incredibly treacherous territory. Longlines have very few defenses from the clever manipulator and can soon end up lying face down with sports car tracks on their backs.

If you choose to pass up a plain and steady Skyline for a hot-looking Bottomline, then you are making a huge mistake. Prepare to be used up and spent. Definitely do not invest a lot of time with a Bottomline. Even a short fling for a sexual rush puts you at great emotional risk. It is wise to avoid this damaging person at all costs. A Bottomline's only hope for finding something resembling a good relationship, a real "match," must be with another strong Bottomline who knows how to play tough and cool.

PICK UP A CRYING BABY

Bottomlines were once precious innocent children, too. That child, in the form of a Bottomline, is now nonexistent. You cannot love someone back to a time of innocence. If a Bottomline has a drop-dead gorgeous face, body, skill or talent, he or she is still emotionally empty inside. Bottomlines live in fear of total rejection if they should ever lose the quality that gains them recognition and attention, confusing that acclaim for love. Now, as adults, they are afraid to lose control, or they might get hurt again, just as they were hurt badly when they were little and vulnerable—the cornerstone of their Bottomline personality.

During conflict with Bottomlines, you will find yourself fighting at their gutter level. These disagreements never reach the higher concepts of mediation or compromise. You must sink to their level to communicate. They will stifle your joy with their disdain. A Bottomline reduces you to screaming fights or perhaps drinks thrown in your face. Worse, such performances are frequently in front of your grieving children. You will be ashamed to participate in such negative confrontations, but that is the best Bottomlines can do. They fight at survival level in every disagreement, just as they did when they were small and desperate.

BUT THEY DON'T REALLY MEAN IT

Often, behind derisive comments made by Bottomlines such as, "You are so fat," you translate the words into a caring thought, like; "You would be healthier if you would exercise." Probably their true thought is, "You should look better for me."

If you think you hear a positive message in cruel comments, then be careful that you are not naively trying to make a silk purse out of a sow's ear. The Bottomline mantra of, "All for me and me for all," compared to the Shortline mantra of, "I am just creating distance, Honey. I need space. I know I can be rude sometimes, yet I love you enough to want you to be healthy," are in completely different categories.

If you are in a relationship with a Bottomline and you have a very long Line or are a Skyline, you may believe you are hearing some message hidden behind all the insults. You want to believe that a Bottomline wants you, even though he or she needs a lot less of you. Remember the difference. A Shortline is not cruel; he or she is well-meaning and blunders a bit with relationships. A

Bottomline is quite heartless.

If you have children, being alone is a healthier alternative. Children receive no benefits from this type of person, and worse, are at risk of becoming emotionally hurt adults because of exposure to your cold Bottomline lover.

Typical of Skylines, you may always love them just a little bit. Skylines sometimes desperately believe that it is enough to be allowed to love, even if you get nothing in return. A love relationship with a Bottomline is mostly fantasy. You never have to stop having warm and loving feelings for Bottomlines, because you threw stellar quality love at them. It is not your fault that your "good love" fell at their feet and then they walked all over it without any appreciation. However, when you get involved with someone who is this selfish, you really need to get therapy help and then probably move on.

Contrast some characteristic Bottomline behavior with Skyline behavior. At a picnic, Bottomlines are the ones to rush to fill their plates without waiting for you. Meanwhile, Skylines are helping to fill elderly people's plates with food. They end up getting their own, now cold, dinner after the desserts have run out. Skylines do not mind giving more than others do. In fact, they hardly notice that they do.

As you acquire greater expertise in **Matchlines Analysis** (self-analysis, clinical analysis of others, body language and deciphering truths and omissions) you will begin to separate the Longlines from the too short ones and the broken ones.

After you interact with individuals that have your Matchline, you will often walk away smiling and feeling better about yourself and life in general. Skylines and Bottomlines can chafe your Line with every interaction, however in very different ways. You often disappoint the Skyline, and the Bottomline is cruel to you.

Stripped of their sports cars and flashy clothes, the shortest of Lines, Bottomlines, are easy to recognize by their selfish behavior. You can look, you may even be tempted to try a bite of forbidden fruit, just keep your distance. The Skyline is a wonderful giver and may just want to love you, but this relationship requires balancing and great sensitivity to keep it from becoming oppressive and hurtful, too.

Love: The irresistible desire to be irresistibly desired."

—Mark Twain

♥

Chapter 10

COMPRESSED DEADLINES
ADDICTIONS AND DEMANDS

*A*ddictive behavior and overwhelming responsibilities can reduce your love capacity severely. Even a Longline will become short with enough pressure.

COMPRESSED LINES

"Compressed Lines" are the result of bad circumstances, not bad childhoods. Compressed Lines are often good people struggling with a surface problem. Compressed Lines may be wonderful in many ways yet emotionally unavailable. Perhaps they are burdened with problems, or married, or restricted because they are grieving over a breakup or a death. Perhaps they are taking care of aging parents, or young children. They are not capable of giving you a full return at this time on your investment of love in them. There is nothing permanently wrong with them; their Line is "compressed."

In all fairness, you deserve a good return on your love now, if that is what you have to offer. A few people are worth waiting for if you believe that they are truly committed. Be certain he or she is not just fooling you into the lose-lose situation of I-take/you-give, and you end up just waiting and waiting with nothing to show for it.

The distinguishing characteristic of a Compressed Line is that once the offending compressor is removed or fixed, then the Line naturally lengthens—not to what its full potential may have been perhaps, but clear gains can be made. The good news is that Compressed Lines can change.

AMANDA AND JOSE

Jose was a man "worth waiting for" his recovery. Amanda did not realize he would return to his old self after he healed.

Jose was handsome, charming, the local soccer star, and well-employed at a large air conditioning firm. His tall blond wife, Amanda, was an efficient computer expert at a medical center. They had a new baby, were in love, and had it made. Jose's parents came from Mexico to visit the new baby. Jose picked them up from the airport. Four blocks from home, a car that ran a stop sign broadsided him.

A month in the hospital, two months of disability and high doses of pain medication left Jose angry, bitter and unpleasant. For Amanda, he was intolerable. She catered to him while carrying her baby on her hip. She loved him and felt sorry for him, but he became so abusive and cold that she left him the moment his back healed enough for him to get around.

When Jose came to therapy, he was embroiled in legal battles over the accident and overwhelmed with hospital bills. Because his wife did not trust him to take care of the baby, she took him to court to restrict overnight visitations. His boss replaced him, and the only pleasure he had was drinking a six-pack and watching soccer on television. He no longer resembled the loving man he had been. He was suffering from depression and severe post-traumatic stress from the car accident.

After a year of rehab, therapy and antidepressants, Jose returned to his former self. He was sober, happy and had a new job.

Unfortunately, Amanda did not wait. She built up so much

resentment from his lashing out at her that she killed any feelings of affection for him. Jose's body healed long before his emotions healed.

Once Amanda understood that Jose was compromised by his physical injuries and by emotional ones as well, she began to soften. She began to trust him again and allowed visitation. Had she understood Matchlines and the compressing effect of the car accident, she might have found patience in her heart to give Jose time to find his lost self. However, the marriage was over. Amanda had lost a good man.

Jose was once a Longline, yet because of the accident, his Line was compressed. He was behaving like a Bottomline, and his wife could not take it. Jose eventually became a Longline again, only some other woman would benefit.

ADDICTIONS

Only the elimination of addictions that compress someone's Line or dedicated Line lengthening personal growth, often including therapy, can effectively lengthen a Line. Addicted people can be deaf, dumb and blind to your genuine love. A full-blown addiction can render the longest Line a Bottomline. Early childhood abuse and character weaknesses often lurk beneath currently addictive lifestyles.

If you are addicted to any substance, please make the call for professional help right now. If a person does not treat the emotional wounds first that are the catalyst for the addiction, the addiction or self-destructive behavior will likely never stop—or sometimes it will just change to a new addiction. Your body may love the substance or behavior. However, do you love your body when you give in to your craving for more of what is expensive, unhealthy, illegal or immoral?

CROSSED LINES

Compressed Line to Longline: *"I'm really trying to quit drinking this time. Please don't go."*

Longline hears: *"Wow. She really needs me. I'd never let her down at a time like this. Don't worry baby, I'm here for you, whatever you need."*

Compressed Line means: *"I need to get him to watch the kids so I can buy a bottle of vodka."*

Remember that the behavior is the symptom, not the cause of any current problems. Unfortunately, people cannot think well if they are using chemicals or acting compulsively. What are their private voices telling them? What is in their distorted thinking process that justifies their bizarre behavior as they self-destruct? Usually the answer is pain and suffering.

Consider the following true example of how one parent's addiction transferred to his child (all examples have identifiers changed to protect confidentiality).

GREG AND HIS DAUGHTER

Greg loved his wife and his daughter. He also loved drugs, all drugs—street, prescription, his wife's medications, whatever he could get. He was out of control for years. Then he began to want more of the good things in life and less of the bad. When he was straight, he was wonderful; when he was high, he was not fun.

He attended Narcotics Anonymous and became stronger. Nevertheless, when he was not using drugs, he heard the drugs like sirens on the seas calling him back. Each time he fell off the wagon, he sickened himself and he lost more self-esteem. He hated that dark hole of drug addiction more and more, whenever he used.

Finally, his wife gave him an ultimatum-he stayed clean or she was gone. She was serious.

Greg did it. He clawed his way out of his compulsive habits and started to enjoy life straight. However, now that he could see more clearly, he noticed something awry. His daughter had grown up while he was busy using drugs, and now she was using them, too. He smelled it on her and saw it in her eyes. Greg told his daughter not to use drugs around him, as it was life or death for him. Instead of quitting drugs, she quit high school and lived where no one cared how many drugs she did.

A grieving and guilt-ridden Greg was at greater risk to use again. He agonized that his daughter was out there unsupervised and vulnerable to the horrible life that he had led. Greg took my advice and brought her home against many recovery principles that would have said to show her tough love. He agreed to allow her to live at home for three months until she finished high school. Without a high school diploma, troubled kids struggle to recover. Greg's daughter needed that one chance not to duplicate her father's life.

On his knees, he asked her why, after what she had seen him go through, she would ever take up doing drugs. The tears flowed as she talked about how frightened she was of her father when he used.

Shocked, he asked her sincerely, "After all the love and care I've given you, why are you afraid of me?"

I asked him, "If a bear attacked you, then stopped for a while to eat berries in the meadow, would you stop being afraid of the bear?"

The look of realization in his eyes of the irreparable damage that happened while he was mentally somewhere else was heart breaking. It only takes one time of violent loss of control to scar a loved one emotionally. Greg and his daughter can talk more openly now. They each are learning to trust again—one trusting reality, and the other trusting her father.

Free To Be Awful

There is a point in a love relationship where one must give up some freedom in the name of compromise to keep a valuable love relationship. This may create trapped, frustrated feelings for addicted Compressed Lines who have high needs for freedom and control. Most Shortlines are uncomfortable with intimacy and get irritated from Longlines' constant asking for more. However, when alcohol or drugs mix with frustration and anger, the common result is violence, warped judgment or crippling indifference and passivity. If your partner chooses drugs or alcohol over family, then he or she may believe that quitting is impossible. An addicted Compressed Line is no longer emotionally available for you or your children.

It is pointless to argue over addicted Compressed Line's hurtful behavior. It will always recur if they do not change their thinking first. That means tons of therapy, just to get to decisions that you might think of as "normal." Conventional treatment tries to control the negative behaviors (symptoms) rather than find the inner pain (the disease). Beneath the addiction layer may be a child who was hurt, never good enough to be loved, mistreated by rigid and abusive parents or much worse.

Sometimes beneath the addictions are people who were once wonderful, but were too weak to survive the hardship of their own lives. If life piles on multiple troubles, traumas and hurts with little or no healing recovery time, then compounding and synergistic damage may occur. As these people continue to be self-destructive, more bad things may happen to them, and the cycle gains momentum. Soon they are whirling waterspouts of disaster pulling you in and down.

You must guard your heart in any relationship that involves an addicted person. Also, remember to guard your work and career, your children, and your money. **Your love cannot mend their pain.** Addictions allow a disengagement from reality. A healthy love relationship requires a clear mind, with an available, emotionally supportive partner, not an anesthetized body in a cloud of stupor. If you are in a relationship with a truly addicted person, then in many ways you are alone emotionally, yet carrying his or her weight on your back.

THE ADDICTIVE LIFESTYLE

Do any of these traits sound familiar to you, or perhaps apply to anyone close to you?

- You need time and privacy to do your addictive behavior
- You hurry through other activities to get back to your drug/behavior
- You travel everywhere with small quantities for your security (flask, joint or one hitter, coffee mug for the car, portable television or hand game, cigarettes, battery vibrator, candy bars, a hit of cocaine)
- Your eyes get a haunted desperate look when you are encouraged or influenced to stop
- Your body hygiene drops, you do not look healthy or happy
- You are alone more often and isolated on purpose.
- You spend more time and funds directed to obtaining the substance or opportunity to practice your addiction
- You consider everything else and everyone else less important
- You select friends who share the addictive behavior; friends who do not have disappeared
- You joke or consider police, parents, spouses, doctors and non-indulging friends as the enemy
- You need the deed as a prerequisite to other fun: smoke a joint before the movie or have a drink before you dance, coke up for the game
- You choose the addiction over other fun activities and important expenditures
- You experience an escalation of dependence as the addiction morphs into the activity itself and becomes the only enjoyable activity: watch porn and masturbate rather than make love to your spouse; smoke pot all day without leaving the house; drink alcohol in front of the television instead of playing ball games
- You become sneaky, hide things, begin to tell lies, all in order to protect the beloved addiction that you say you hate
- You use anger, blame, and frustration to cover up shame and guilt over the deed

Natalie And Her Mom

Natalie tried to love her boyfriend after he became a daily pot smoker, but he would not let her.

Natalie was a nineteen-year-old college student, whose relationship with her boyfriend ended because he lied to her about secretly buying illegal drugs. Natalie was desperately trying to win him back, on the condition that he would stop using any drugs. She was showing up where he played in his band and was even checking his e-mail to see if he had another girlfriend. She would alternate between whining for him to come back to her and getting angry with him. Naturally, he was avoiding her like the plague.

Natalie came to me because she was also having trouble with her mother, who was suffering from the empty nest syndrome and besieging Natalie with phone calls. Natalie was considering transferring to a college out of state to get away from her mother.

I drew the Matchlines for Natalie so that she could see that she was in the same Line position with her mother as her boyfriend was with her. Natalie had grown up and no longer needed smothering by her mother. Natalie's boyfriend had dropped out and now met his needs with drugs instead of her. Both Natalie and her mother were rejected for trying to love someone like they had successfully done in the past.

Suddenly she felt compassion for her mother's achy heart. Natalie decided to arrange to spend one afternoon each week with her mom, doing whatever she wanted, on the condition that her mother agreed to take one college course with Natalie. Natalie would be weaning her mother away from her while helping her to find other interests.

Natalie could see by the Matchlines that her boyfriend was not holding out on her. She realized that her boyfriend's Line was initially short and additionally compressed by the drug use. Based on his relationship history, he could not treat her with kindness, or friendship. It was normal for him to deceive her and break up with her coldly. She decided to stop pressuring him for a relationship that was impossible for him to give to her, especially while he continued to use drugs.

Natalie asked her boyfriend to talk to her on the telephone twice per week to help her find a little relief from her pain until her broken heart healed. He agreed to this and became less defensive the more she backed away. They established a distant friendship, and in time, Natalie began dating someone new, someone who had a longer Line.

A first-love loss is difficult. Natalie required nearly six months to grieve, but the desperate struggle between Natalie and the people she loved ended peacefully and compassionately.

RELATIONSHIP NOT THE PERSON

Learn to separate in your mind the "relationship" itself from the person with whom you are having the relationship. Depending on the emotional shape of your partner, you could have a very different relationship with him or her if you met five years ago or five years from now. Any relationship can become distorted, abusive and very unhealthy. Yet, the person that you are involved with may be a wonderful person with all kinds of fine qualities. Because of specific behaviors that established the rules of your relationship, bad habits may have developed that now have the potential to escalate into an unhealthy relationship for both of you.

If you continue to focus on the "person," then you must admit that person has many redeeming qualities. You could list many good reasons why you should stay with your partner in spite of your misery.

Instead, if you can focus on the "relationship" that you are having right now, and ask yourself, "Am I growing? Am I feeling good in this relationship? Or is it restricting me, dominating me, or making me feel sad?"

If you conclude that you are in a bad relationship, then you need to either leave it, or find the tools to change the relationship. You do not have to stop loving this person, enjoying this person, or even having safe sex with him or her—whatever part of the relationship you must keep until you move on. However, if it is truly hurtful, then you do need to stop the exclusivity of the relationship and separate physically from your partner. That may require great courage if you fear "being alone."

"Love cannot endure indifference. It needs to be wanted. Like a lamp, it needs to be fed out of the oil of love, or the flame burns low."
—Henry Ward Beecher

♥

Chapter 11

COMPRESSED OUTLINES
BODY AND SOCIAL

A body image that appears to be socially non-conforming can be a significant compressor. Anything that differs from society's "norm," such as being too short, too tall, too light, too dark, too little, too big, can be devastating emotionally if it began as a childhood source of shame. This is most damaging during the teen years. Often, appearances matter too much to children due to peer pressure and superficial values.

Adolescent bodies grow and develop erratically and often create self-loathing that can last a lifetime. Natural bodily functions like perspiration, menstruation, erections, urination and breath odor are sources of shame and embarrassment. Nervous laughter, tasteless jokes or whispers are indications of discomfort with our bodies rather than a relaxed comfort with being human and "like everyone else."

WAISTLINES

Regardless of your actual looks, if people tell you repeatedly that you are too "something," you will probably believe it. However, people gain influence and power over you only when you give it to them and allow others to dominate or humiliate you. As a child, you may not have the power to stop other people, but as an adult, you can change your opinion of yourself right now. Redefine your image as you want it to be, first in your own mind, and then in other people's perception of who you are.

CHRIS' TROUBLES

Chris was tall and dark, but not handsome. He was awkward like all teenagers and preteens in their approach to the opposite sex. Chris would overcompensate for his shy sensitivity with a bold and usually overtly sexual come on.

Equally shy, the girls turned their backs on him and consistently said, "No thanks."

Chris would stare at himself in the mirror and rip what was left of his self-esteem to shreds. He would berate himself for his exotic looks and blamed his failures on his features.

Soon he approached every girl as if he were approaching a battlefield. Chris was also abnormally assertive, irresistibly curious and sharp-witted. Had he been a stunner with Ivy League looks, his other qualities would have still intimidated young girls.

He began to hate, as well as love, girls for his dependence and for their control over him. If he did persuade a woman to be with him, then it was only to use her sexually as a conquest. He blamed all women for his early rejections and became addicted to "scoring." He used his face as an excuse not to improve in other areas. Because he could not change his looks, he became a defeatist with all women. He sold out on himself.

He could have made many positive changes to make himself more attractive. Chris could have turned the heat down on his approach and learned to sweet-talk in place of caustic sarcasm. He allowed his own negative body image to dictate the next thirty years of his life. Eventually with therapy, he learned to feel good enough as he is. He became successful, and soon started to value his character and other good qualities over superficial looks.

Body images acquired when we are at our worst in adolescence can linger. The haunting images of awkwardness can remain mentally locked as shameful memories of inadequacies. If you have residual childhood body images that scream "not good enough," regardless of what you look like, it is time to grow up and away from all of it.

Phat Not Fat

Advertising specialists know how to program the human mind. With art and humor, the media programs our subconscious to buy associated products as well as to emulate stars. The current "ideal" body image portrayed today is not healthy for men or women. A censorship of anorexic and chemically or surgically altered role models remains the responsibility of the audience and the producer of the shows. Awareness of eating disorder clinics or hearing a seven-year-old say that she is fat might help to raise a producer's conscience. Perhaps, people just might identify with, and buy the products sold by a rosy-cheeked face or a muscular form of normal weight more readily than an emaciated model or a drugged-out looking persona. Fortunately, for the little girls' and young boys' health, our consumer dollars speak loudly and always have the final say.

Gender Compressors

The making of an American "man" creates a shorter Line in many males. Studies show that parents and caretakers pick up less, nurture less, kiss less and talk with less to their young boys than they do with young girls. Even teachers treat male children differently than female students. Are boys' lines made shorter, perhaps, due to a parental homophobic fear that is so strong that they overcompensate and are often cold, or even cruel to little boys?

Is it possible our society deprives boys of reaching their full potential in premeditated and calculated socialization processes? Higher demands, with fewer needs met, make cold-hearted and mean puppies so why not little children? By age twelve, many male children are so negatively socialized that they often seek violence. They begin to reject both family and affection. If this process is successful, then future wives and children will suffer by association with cold, violent individuals.

How do you treat your sons? Did your parents treat your brothers differently than they did you? How do you feel when boys cry or act tenderly? Do you react differently to friends walking hand in hand if they are boys...or girls?

GIRLS ARE FOR...?

In the past, men often valued women solely on their looks. Some rebels managed to recover from this, and they stopped shaving their legs or wearing stilettos. Others feel compelled to resort to a cosmetic surgeon. Some people judge any deviation from the perfect American pin-up a "deformity," rather than special "uniqueness." Low self-esteem is rarely based in reality. Overheard or self-created, low self-esteem is a result of cruel jokes, comments or comparisons. Soon the child believes she or he is abnormal.

Ironically, the most attractive women often suffer from the poorest body images. Pretty women are not valued for what they can do; rather they are overvalued for their appearance. This renders them passive and powerless to determine their own fate as they become dependent on pleasing others' eyes. Self-esteem must come from the choices you make, your integrity, and what you do and think of your actions, not on others' opinions. Inflated self-esteem collapses when based solely on outside opinions and flattery.

Women's self-esteem is often limited by the time they are nine or ten years old if they listen to jokes that victimize women, or compare themselves to impossible standards. People in control of money and power have historically devalued women.

How much of your day do you spend trying to be attractive when you could be out having fun? If you were a completely financially independent female, would you curl your eyelashes and fight every day to weigh 120 pounds? On the other hand, would you play more, explore and get dirty and messy learning new skills? How could you spend the time differently that you now spend to look the way society dictates that you should look?

Recent social pressure on men to look "ripped" is contributing to less self-confidence in males and more shame about their bodies, just like girls.

SOCIAL COMPRESSORS

On a social level, big events that happen in our society can damage an individual's ability to trust and love freely. As networks fill the twenty-four hours news demand, our bodies react with pain and empathy as we learn of shocking, worldwide events. The media plays a duel role, first inflaming the injury to a horrific personal level, and second through overexposure, contributing to a desensitizing and de-humanizing process as we try to avoid feeling grief. All designed to keep a captive audience.

Grief has distinct stages, as described by Kubler-Ross, including bargaining, anger and acceptance. The way that you handle grief and loss is a primary measure of mental health. Prolonged grief can destroy the quality of your life.

Will anyone more than fifty years old recover from watching television the weekend the president of the United States, John F. Kennedy, was murdered; the people's princess, Princess Diana, lost in a car wreck; the children slaughtered by other children in their Columbine schoolrooms; the Robert Kennedy and Martin Luther King assassinations? Will the elderly ever recover from the world wars? Will our own children recover from the media's coverage of the 9/11 terrorist acts or close-up footage of recent wars every night?

These events are social compressors that become personalized tragedies for individuals and thus create shortened Lines for society as a whole. The media replays these tragedies at every opportunity. Just in case you start to heal, the media does an annual recap. Such emotional trips are not necessary. More importantly, the stressful input is so prolific our psyches simply cannot take it. Too often, we are powerless to turn off the noise, and thus, never have time to recover. This is particularly true for our children.

MEDIA MATTERS

Does the barrage of media, music and movie violence create an anonymous, numb, and thereafter, an amoral, if not immoral, society? Are we spawning cold-blooded, desensitized and disconnected children with limited conscience or knowledge of right or wrong? The innocent children do not know what is best for them, and they are most often the ones who suffer from social mistakes. Children are clean slates until we mold them.

The difficulty is establishing the line between protecting freedom of speech for adults and the protection of developing minds that could be permanently warped by relentless negative input. Without the entertainment industry, the news, musicians, writers and actors taking any responsibility or personal accountability, the task to protect children falls on overwhelmed parents alone. The time-proven village concept of child rearing has lost favor. In the past, large families and extended families contributed to the raising of a child. Now a child's relatives may be a thousand miles away as families spread out globally.

Millions of children are exposed to popular and revered stars in their roles of thieves, killers, or the sexually confused. Does greed for money or fame takes precedence over societal obligation, and at what point does someone become a co-conspirator to childhood brain washing? While that concept may not hold up in a court of law, as parents of suicidal children have learned after attempting to sue various artists, the moral imperative and responsibility is still there.

Children are always watching and often demand adult privileges. Even the children of the musicians and actors are vulnerable to damage by their own parent's participation in the plethora of sex and violence. America protects all forms of freedom of speech. Indeed, people are eager to have every right and freedom to express themselves. However, the necessary maturity and responsibility needed to accompany such privileges are absent in children.

Every day you are programming your little computer brain with bits of spam that you could block. Soon you are so fried you cannot even question the quality or the truth of what you are watching. Controlling brain-deadened masses is easier than you might imagine and facilitates the flourishing of corrupt leaders.

Whenever possible, try to limit the amount of entertainment and world news that you allow to become emotionally incorporated into your grieving psyche. If you believe that your Line has been shortened by political, social or peer negativity, try turning off the violence and crisis-based news. You can listen to the summaries of national news infrequently, and still maintain an informed status.

It may take time to heal and have feelings of compassion again. How about spending your money on wholesome and entertaining movies that tell a good story with characters that you admire?

HEAL

Let go of most of the trouble and sorrow surrounding you so that you have time to heal as a human being. Otherwise, you will become unfeeling as a natural defense against such negativity before you even know or realize it happened. On an individual level, every experience with grief walls us up a little tighter as we protect our "emotional bellies" from assault. The result is a lack of room for love and childlike joy. We become numb and dulled by the experience, deadened, less childlike, less innocent, more emotionally closed up and defensive. Love cannot get through to you, and certainly, less love comes from you.

Multiple losses, betrayals, and lies are happening somewhere in the world constantly. However, we are not built physically and mentally to carry the stress-weight of everyone's pain on our individual shoulders. It is not your job to bear the weight of the whole world. Rather, if you choose sanity and peacefulness over knowing it all, you may come to "know yourself" on a much deeper level.

The next chapter deals with the most difficult personalities. Although our Lines are shortened by observing social trauma, personal experience with trauma can cause a child's Line to "break" into a **Faultline**. Personal **trauma**— personal experience in war, emotional or physical abuse, a highly-conflicted and acrimonious home, severe grief, or neglect, can be extremely potent and damaging to your Line. The damage is likely in inverse proportion to a person's age when the trauma occurred, (younger is usually worse) and is proportionate to both the severity and duration of the trauma. You cannot love away someone's traumatic history after very early childhood, nor unravel the fabric of someone's core belief system. You can only recognize it and decide how you choose to deal with it.

Unfortunately, people with Faultlines experienced factors that compromised their love capacity so severely that dysfunction and skewed judgment now exist in their relationships. **There is a world of difference between a Compressed Line and someone with a Faultline.** If someone is temporarily compressed, he or she might be worth waiting for—until after recovery. The person with a significant Faultline is unlikely to recover without intense therapy for many years and may be a hidden danger to your mind and heart. Only with hard committed work can a person with a Faultline salvage himself or herself into becoming a healthy partner.

"*You can give without loving, but you can't love without giving.*"

—Amy Carmichael

Chapter 12
FAULTLINES
DOORMATS AND TAKERS

Some people have cleverly learned to deceive and to control people with **ingratiating behavior.** These pseudo-Longlines can conceal emotional damage that privately behind the closed door of your bedroom rears its ugly face worse than any spoiled Bottomline. These individuals are selfish, a lot like the Bottomline, and they often have mental problems that make them very dangerous to love.

The Bottomline will break your heart; however, someone with a Faultline can also break your spirit, rob you of your sanity and then blame you for everything. They may be generous with their money or donate hours to charities, and are very careful to manage assignments. Yet, when you interact with them, you feel stung, obligated and apologetic, and you do not know why. You soon think something is wrong with you. However, in reality, something is very wrong with them. You see, people with Faultlines were psychologically broken as children.

Faultlines: A Good Front

People with Faultlines want their partner to appear happy. They may act in most ways like someone with a long Line. However, Longlines give love freely and innocently. Faultlines have an agenda, a plan for their partners that benefits only them. Faultlines will criticize until there is nothing left of their partner's self-esteem. In their mind, the normal partner is a threat that needs controlling. This may escalate to the point of sadistic control.

Broken Belief Systems

Trauma creates Faultlines—complete splits or cracks that effectively shorten the length of Lines. Wherever that fault or crack appears on the Line, then that is the true length of the Line, no matter how well someone may try to mask it or pretend otherwise. The result is a faulted way of thinking—a severe glitch, a break in the line—a skewed way a person reasons through problems and conflicts.

Unfortunately, if you changed in every way Faultlines may ask of you, they still would not like you or be satisfied with you. A person with a Faultline struggles terribly and may not love you in a healthy way; however, he or she does need you to lean on in order to feel good about him or herself. When Faultline partners continue to feel empty inside, they resent you, and may punish you for not being able to fix their pain. Faultlines are not capable of healing from their past traumas without help. Faultlines need therapy.

Cynthia And Rob

Cynthia was a freshman in college when she met Rob. Rob was a graduate student, handsome and charming. They were married quickly and a child soon followed.

Rob began to leave Cynthia a list that she was to complete. If she did not complete her tasks on the list, she was not allowed to eat dinner. The lists grew longer and more difficult to accomplish. Rob enjoyed sadistic games at night, and then by day, he was exemplary at work, social engagements and church.

Cynthia's mother dropped by, and Cynthia daringly told her part of what was transpiring. Her mother thought her young daughter was exaggerating and being dramatic. Now a nervous wreck, Cynthia went to see her priest.

The priest admonished her and sternly told her the Bible said to obey her husband, who, in his estimation, was clearly a wonderful man.

Rob became even sicker, and began to starve Cynthia. He had the phone removed and threatened to harm her and the baby if she spoke to anyone. One day, she visited her mother, and miraculously, somehow ended up in my office that day.

Her body shook with spasms as she told her story. She did not return to Rob. Instead, still terrified, she divorced him. She could neither speak nor lift her head in court, much less tell the judge the truth about him. I made certain that the judge knew the child's side of the story that included the gruesome details. The judge ordered supervised visitation for Rob. Cynthia's son grew up to be a wonderful and talented man. I learned years later that Rob's next girlfriend "fell down" at his home and became severely brain damaged. Rob gave a sad report to the police and the case was closed.

Faultlines hope desperately that you can somehow repair their childhood damage. You cannot fix them. This all leads to cycles of criticism and disdain that could destroy you, and never help them. Do not buy into this lethal game. They need **professional** help.

BAD PARENTS

Dysfunctional families have chronic problems that do not allow a child to have a normal childhood. Some parents were inept and inexperienced because they were too young when they had children. Tragically, some used reverse reinforcement (the good are beaten, the bad are rewarded) that may simply have stemmed from ignorance. Reversed reinforcement is all too common in privileged families too busy to give time, so parents buy off their children regardless of their behavior, creating a nightmare of a human being.

Some children are hurt or severely abused beyond recovery. A person with a Faultline can sometimes be the result of molestation, cruel or neglectful parents, a personality disorder or a brain chemical imbalance in the child or the parent as well as many other things. Permanent Faultline breaks may come from severe childhood trauma or fears, or multiple traumas occurring too close together.

Chip Off The Ole Block

Mentally ill parents who are clinically depressed, alcoholic, addicted, neglectful, manic depressive or schizophrenic may have offspring who have faults in their Lines (unfair and tragic for perfect babies to be so badly programmed by unfortunate and troubled parents). These compromised parents often have one or more failed marriages that expose their children to grief and loss, and multiple stepparents that only exacerbate the damage.

To meet basic survival and acceptance needs, these children began to manipulate and control those around them to endure their sometimes-horrific environments. As children, they learned that their feelings and needs were not important to others, and that feelings of love and caring were rarely reciprocal. Consequently, personality disorders may surface, perhaps in the form of the self-centered narcissist or the alienated schizoid. Internment, torture, kidnapping, rape, jail and prison camps can create Faultlines in adults, who if untreated, will tend to break under future pressure. They are often driven, yet, internally frightened people who must succeed, but are ill equipped to lead.

Someone else cannot mend or love away a fault in a Line. Emotional scars will predictably have an effect on future behavior. **Sincerely motivated people can make progress with therapy to undo this damage.** Unfortunately, people with Faultlines often can neither see nor admit to their damage, because on the outside they appear functional, even successful. On the inside, they wrongly convince themselves that they are Longlines and that their actions are completely justified. Therefore, obviously, you must be the problem, not them.

But wait! Faultline thinking is often distorted.

A person with a Faultline typically has very predictable, illogical, recurrent, destructive behavior patterns whenever the pressure in a relationship begins to rise. Imagine a reward system gone wrong. If a drunk or crazy keeper gives a lab pigeon pellet rewards in unpredictable senseless patterns, the pigeon will learn confusion, frustration, rage and the need to control the craziness. Pity the new keeper who must retrain the bird's now mysterious illogical behavior. Are you the new keeper for a person with a Faultline who is acting "crazy?" Unfortunately, they may have also hated the people they wanted to love.

Emotional pain and fear can be so overwhelming that a need to compensate or cover often arises. A tendency toward addictions and obsessive/compulsive behaviors begins to surface as a protective barrier. These skewed behaviors become personality disorders and addictions, and without treatment, become permanent glitches in their Line.

A personality "glitch," like this creates two distinct types of people with Faultlines, called either "Doormats" or "Takers." They become either desperate people-pleasers or worse, emotionally skewed.

FAULTLINE DOORMATS

The desperate people-pleaser may appear to be just an overly needy Longline. It appears that they just want to be close to you. Remember a Skyline is unselfish with no agenda. However, Faultline Doormats will sacrifice until they bleed, and then resent you for not doing the same thing for them, all with the intention to manipulate you. Most often Faultline Doormats are women, because girls are often encouraged in our society to be passive. Obsessive giving, caretaking and invasive "fixing" are common indications of a Faultline Doormat **and** of a Skyline mom. The difference is that the Faultline Doormat uses the guilt and kindness of others to control them in a malicious, non-loving way. Skyline mom's just love to give.

Like all people with Faultlines, who were hurt earlier in life by their dangerous environments, Faultline Doormats feel they must stay in control. Eventually, frustrating rejection feels normal to them, and in spite of your protests, they desperately attempt to ingratiate themselves into your life. They offer to take care of your pets, or kids, or run your errands. It feels unsettling, but you cannot quite put your finger on the problem. They seem so nice!

CROSSED LINES

Doormat says to Longline: *"Take your time finding a job. You can stay with me and I'll pay for everything until you get on your feet."*

Longline says to Doormat: *"How incredibly nice of you. How about we share use of my car since yours is broken down?"*

Doormat Means: *"No, I don't want fairness; I need you to be dependent on me. I will sacrifice and then you will owe me favors and I can manipulate you with guilt. This is just what I wanted."*

Underneath the Doormat's niceness is fear, an emotional glitch. You might sense it, however, probably too late. By then they will have your house key, know too much about you, or be flirting with your spouse before you realize that they have a Faultline and that you are in danger.

Remember, a true Longline or Skyline gives unselfishly. They are not looking for payback. They are happy just to adore you. Love is not so simple with Doormats. Faultline Doormats want you to owe them, so they keep you beholden to them all the while **appearing** subservient to you. That is their way of keeping you under control and them in power.

HIDDEN AGENDA

You may find Faultline Doormats volunteering at church, helping in the classroom and hospitals. They can quote the Good Books, their boss or any of several well-known experts to justify their actions at any time. Because he or she always acts so caring in public, no one believes you when you say the

Doormat did something mean. They often stab you with a disguised dagger. Maybe this behavior is the little trade off they ask for, or maybe they will lose your paperwork, or forget to relay your message. If you catch them in their little game, they will surely make a scene.

The Faultline Doormat might even self-mutilate just to make you feel guilty! Have you known people who threaten to kill themselves if you try to end a relationship? They will cry and tell everyone what you said, milking it for every drop of attention and sympathy. Of course, you will just look bad as you crawl away defeated and confused.

Remember, their behavior is fear-based. **In their thinking, if a Doormat with a Faultline can control and manipulate you, then you are less likely to hurt them.**

FAULTLINE TAKER

Faultline Takers are so emotionally withdrawn and self-centered that you feel like a big truck ran over you when they "love" you. When you complain, they withdraw, punishing you. Abusive Faultline Takers are often involved with other people only so that they can get an edge on them, control them and stay a few steps above them. They use a desperate "pulley-system" to keep control and always win—that is, they can only go up when you are going down. They can only feel good if they believe someone else feels worse than they do—and that person is usually going to be you.

Their self-centeredness sees only your failure to love them enough to make it all better, so they hate you and bully you, demanding you do more for them before they do anything for you. Their powerlessness ends up as rage. If they are angry about their job, parents, or ex-spouse—even though you cannot fix any of it for them—you will end up suffering for it.

Even with complete submission by their partner, Faultline Takers are not satisfied. You can give them everything, and they will still want more. Sometimes their need feels like hot love, but they need you only in ways that eventually hurt you.

Faultline Takers strive to succeed as if their lives depended on it. They stay maniacally busy, so buried trauma memories never catch up with them. These hurt people are very concerned with what the next person is thinking, because as children their lives depended upon correctly reading an adult's state of mind.

In dangerous households, children may sincerely believe their lives are at risk. In violent, scary, households their lives may in fact depend on knowing what a parent is thinking at any given moment. Healthy, independent people typically do not worry about other people's thoughts; rather, they are busy living their own life. They are free from trauma-based behavior so prevalent in a Taker.

A Faultline Taker also cannot tolerate an independent act by you. You have become "out of control and dangerous." If you do something independent, they are not happy for you, and retaliate twice as punishing as you might expect. This can also escalate to verbal and even physical abuse.

The Faultline Taker will criticize, rather than celebrate your successes. Eventually, just to avoid the Faultline Taker's displeasure, you curtail all your activities until you become static to the point of waiting your whole life away in case they summon you. You are afraid to get them riled up over a shopping trip or a visit to a friend. Soon you have no life of your own and are completely unattractive to yourself, others, and even to the Faultline Taker. They, in turn, do not like what they have created. So do not think you please them by letting them control you. They will despise you, and you will be sinking to the level of their fractured Line.

In addition, keep in mind, Faultline Takers have the potential to hurt and damage whoever they are near—not just you. They are in great emotional pain and fear their own destructive behavior. Many of them turn to an addictive behavior to escape their fear and pain. Protect your children and pets.

Others mask their problems with rigid, socially appropriate behavior that "looks good" to other people. Many of them are heads of corporations, law or medical practices, run major projects, or rise high in the military and political arenas. They dress right, have good haircuts and are often quite successful in business and finances. Many of them are workaholics. This makes them more difficult to spot because they are doing positive things, and so, outwardly, they appear to be very self-disciplined and often quite successful. However, ask someone who has tried to love a controlling Faultline what he or she is really like. Get close to a Faultline Taker and you will run into barbed wire around a cold heart.

CROSSED LINES

> **Longline says to Taker:** *"Honey, guess what? I just got that big promotion I was up for!"*
>
> **Taker says to Longline:** *"Darling, that's wonderful. However, I have decided that I do not want you to work. The children need you at home."*
>
> **Taker means:** *"I am so threatened by your success that there's no way I'm going to be supportive. You might leave me."*

In the following case, Libby was a patient who learned to see through the slick facade of someone with a Faultline by observing the man's wife:

LIBBY AND THE DEAN

Libby worked for a small junior college in Nebraska. The new dean arrived from the East with his ultra-sophisticated secretary in tow. They were perfect looking, charming, and efficient. Libby felt poorly dressed and inadequate when she introduced herself to them at the college's welcoming tea. She noticed a withered-looking woman off to herself and was shocked to discover she was the dean's wife of twenty years. Her weak smile and lowered chin reminded Libby of the demeanor of a beaten dog.

What could such a great person like the new dean see in a partner like this? Libby herself was secretly attracted to the dean's powerful persona.

Later that year Libby was confused when the dean did not keep agreements that he had made about Libby's classes or her salary increase. Libby was quite sure that she remembered correctly and tried to argue her case. She could not believe the dean would lie to her. Libby was a good teacher, yet her contract was not renewed. What had she done wrong?

The truth was later discovered that the dean was selfish and deceitful. He misappropriated funds; he lost his position at the college in disgrace, and he moved on, taking his glamorous secretary and pitiful wife with him.

Thankfully, Libby had not become romantically involved with the dean. She foolishly trusted him because he looked good, was successful and acted like a winner. He was none of these. Had she given in to her desire for the dean, then she would be brokenhearted as well as jobless. Libby learned the hard way that often the face of a spouse or a child tells you volumes about the inner character of a Faultline.

Be observant. True Longlines treat their partners, children, friends and pets like royalty.

WHAT ARE YOU THINKING?

A person with a Faultline lacks the capacity to be genuinely intimate in a committed way. As if observing from afar, they are detached from whom they are. This detachment is often the result of a trauma that caused too much anguish with which the child could cope. For example, if a child has a severe trauma, such as the loss of a family member in a car wreck, the experience is usually repressed, hidden down deep inside. Like a computer with surge protection, when trauma is so big that it might endanger the mind, the body attempts to save itself. Memory fails in order to prevent a meltdown. The child quickly resumes his or her laughing and playing, and never mentions the incident again unless forced to do so. Do not be fooled by the appearance of normalcy. Some damage is permanently there.

Faultlines tend to be very polarized. Either they stop valuing themselves completely (Doormats) or they learn to value only themselves (Takers). There is no balance. They work very hard at keeping themselves emotionally separated from you. In a relationship, when you have needs, they pull away. As part of their defensive wall, they must maintain an image of normalcy, so they tend to donate generously their time and money to others. This inevitably makes you think the problem must be you.

It is not you.

Faultlines may pursue you romantically because you enhance their image. They will take you to the right parties, but are unavailable if you need them emotionally for a parent's funeral, or if dealing with conflicts that require responsibility for their half of the relationship. They may say all the right words to convince you both of their desire for you and of their sincerity. Yet hidden inside lingers locked-up pain that they have not yet been willing to confront. You cannot make them deal with such pain. They need professional help if any healing is still possible.

They will say, "My Dad beat me and left when I was nine, and I was glad. It didn't affect me." The damage is typically repressed. Trauma always causes deep hurt and emotional damage.

People with Faultlines function well in society, yet when alone with you can be very cold and blocked. You may feel the ice water on your happy little heart as they explain logically and in detail why you are always the problem. People who have been hurt have power and control needs that can only be satisfied by controlling weaker people or by dropping out completely. The long-term effect of chronic rejection and undeserved criticism is that you begin to feel as if you are repulsive and a little crazy. Perhaps a partner with a Faultline told you that you would be undesirable to a future lover. Cover your ears. You may run the risk of feeling trapped with an unmatched partner because he or she will convince you that he or she is the **best** you will ever do. Therefore, you stay with the frightened, insecure person with a Faultline.

The following story illustrates the moment a patient realized her husband had a Faultline:

Gina And Tom

Gina's heart was breaking. As she dressed for her dear father's funeral, her ribs seemed to close in around her lungs. She had to sit down on her bed to breathe.

Gina's husband, Tom, dressed quickly and waited downstairs. At the funeral, Tom was the perfect host, thanking each guest personally, shaking hands and looking sincerely into each guest's eyes. Observing him from the side, Gina reached for the hand of her best friend, Lottie. Tom had not held her nor spent any time with her since the news of her father's death. Although he had not been close to her father, he was receiving the lion's share of comforting and kind words from her father's influential friends. Tom did not even look Gina's way.

Gina wondered if her distorted, grief-stricken face signaled everyone to tiptoe around her. Everyone, that is, except Lottie. Lottie did not even care when Gina's tears stained her new silk blouse. Lottie knew how to be close when someone needed her.

Tom seemed like the perfect husband, however, he was terrified of the raw emotions Gina was experiencing and he wanted none of it. He was not willing to make himself uncomfortable for her, even in her moment of greatest need. With great effort, he took time to pat Gina's shoulder, and then quickly moved away. The funeral guests smiled approvingly and joined him on the other side of the room. Gina could still feel his icy fingers as she took her place in the front pew.

Gina needed comforting and her husband was incapable of delivering. Tom would never recognize his deficits nor admit to them because someone with a Faultline cannot recognize his own distorted behavior. Tom would swear he was perfect at the funeral. He might even have convinced Gina—had she not already seen and understood the concept of Matchlines.

WEAK AND RIGID

People with Faultlines leave the hard duty of emotions to you because they do not want anything penetrating their protective shell. They are afraid and defensive. They are never people with strength of character that you can depend upon, even though they may be strict, cruel or rigid. Generally, they are weak and cowardly, maybe even broken people whom therapy could help compassionately.

Rather than pity or emulate partners with a Faultline, suggest they need help. Emotional stuff is too dangerous for them so they will reject your first suggestions vehemently. They excuse themselves when things get tough. The happy child in them is locked down tight. Any kindness may be just for show, or if it is a sincere gesture, then it will disappear quickly when they feel threatened. You feel empty and cold in their arms because, in many ways, they are like emotional mirages.

Sometimes people with Faultlines appear to act just like Longlines because they will spend excessive "quality" time with you. Unlike Longlines, they will spend that time controlling you, making you feel guilty, and hurting your feelings. Be alert for signs of a major past trauma like a history of molestation. Their fractured Lines can cross over yours and wrap themselves around you, obsessing about you. That can be a sign of desperate mental illness—not true love-behavior. They can choke the life out of you while explaining the fault is all yours. They need you to make themselves whole. They cannot love you back in the condition they are in right now. If you do have sincere love for them, then step back and insist that they attend long-term professional therapy.

Consider the difference: Bottomlines may betray you and not care if they hurt you. They do not love you enough. Bottomlines use you and move on rather quickly. Faultlines may betray you, but cleverly blame you for their bad behavior. They fear losing you, nevertheless, they treat you awfully and keep you right next to them, a prisoner to punish and mess up your mind.

Really, when Faultlines are not using you, they would rather that you did not bother them, lest you do something image tarnishing. If so, then you are disciplined and left alone again. They would prefer you to do things from a distance, unless they accompany you only to supervise, and rarely to participate. You run the risk of getting in trouble here, because you may be getting attention only for negative behavior. Longlines married to people with Faultlines sometimes live in lonely, ivory towers.

The following case exemplifies a destructive family and a person with a Faultline who badly misused a confused woman.

TASHA'S STAR

Tasha lived in the shadow of her celebrity husband. In the magazine photographs, he was doting and affectionate, with his arms wrapped around her. At home, she could do nothing right.

He was cold and cruel and nothing pleased him. He was the star and the breadwinner, and he wanted her to be quiet and content.

Tasha began an affair with her husband's best friend out of spite and hatred for his cruelty. She rarely enjoyed the sex and referred to the affair as revenge sex. When her mother-in-law discovered the liaison and told Tasha's husband, he was livid. He struck her and verbally abused her. Yet, he talked to her for hours about their problems, and made passionate love with her nearly every night for two weeks. He wanted to reinstate his control and power over her.

Tasha could not believe the reaction she was getting and thought, mistakenly, that he must really love her. As soon as he felt he had her under his control again, he returned to ignoring her.

In public, he was the ever-doting husband. Tasha could not bear his indifference and sought out increasingly inappropriate lovers— her husband's banker, and then her gardener—the true "desperate housewife." She was secretly hoping her husband would catch her just so he would notice her.

Eventually, her reputation was in ruins, her self-esteem fell so low that she attempted to kill herself with a drug overdose. Her behavior was dysfunctional, demeaning to herself and desperate. All she wanted was his love and attention. No one suspected that her husband was the reason for her despair because he appeared so caring.

He had the full support of his friends and family. He even poured his heart out to her friends. Tasha had no one left. Tasha eventually was no longer useful to him and he let her go. Because of all the mistakes that she had made, she felt that she had to leave town. Her husband made sure she left without any of his plentiful assets.

All she ever wanted was love, yet he had nothing to give her except a fake image, a hologram of love.

THE RIVER REVERTS TO ITS ORIGINAL COURSE

Once a person with a Faultline enters an adult love relationship and fails, the disappointment and failure will be crushing for both partners. You can bet your house and life savings on the fact that people with Faultlines will crash repeatedly, frequently failing you emotionally. Without intensive therapy, they may only make a dent in their distorted belief system, even if they want to change with all their heart. Understanding and believing that they have a glitch in their Line that fails is their best chance to begin to interact with partners on a less destructive level.

If you decide to love a person with a Faultline—and it is your decision—then you need to be prepared to be hurt often.

ABUSE

A relationship with a person with a Faultline or with a Bottomline is typically an abusive relationship. When an abusive relationship begins, the highs and lows start small. There is no indication that this relationship is any different from any other developing relationship with compromises and some problems. What begins to differentiate an abusive relationship from one that is normal is a recurring one-sidedness of selfish behavior. Your partner's selfish behavior is like a blow that strikes you. Concerned only with his or her own interests, your partner hurts you for trying to commit to the relationship.

The waves of "highs and lows" begin to get larger. The hurts are more frequent and deeper. The honeymoon period follows when your partner tries to heal all your wounds and make everything temporarily all right. However, the dysfunctional partner inevitably returns to their abusive and selfish acts. This creates an addiction in the abused party, like the rush of heroin and the agony of withdrawal.

When two different types of people with Faultlines, a Taker and a Doormat get together, though technically well-matched, the struggle for absolute power often escalates to abusive levels. Intervention often fails because they feed off each other's weak, sick behavior and the relationship is a long-lasting nightmare.

FIRST TIMERS

Longlines who has never been in an abusive relationship before will generally fail to recognize the beginning fluctuations when involved with a new Bottomline or Faultline lover. They often think that these flip-flops are a result of normal conflicts in the relationship. Longlines are quite surprised when their partners suddenly blame them. Faultlines say that their partner is the reason they did selfish, mean things.

If you had been home for their phone call, they would not have gone out drinking with friends for days. If you had confronted your boss more and landed a better job, then they would not have had to drain your bank account. If you had not received a parking ticket, they would not have punched you

CROSSED LINES

> **Longline to Friend:** *"Oh my gosh! Brad came over at midnight Friday, and we made love on my dining room table! Late dates are so hot!"*
>
> **Friend to Longline:** *"Sounds exciting. But where was he before midnight, and have you heard from him since? It's Wednesday, ya know."*
>
> **Longline to Friend:** *"Oh, he was at some work party. Besides, he said he was super busy. He told me to wait for his call."*

Longlines have a lot of love in their hearts and a lot of forgiveness. They can be very introspective. They may begin to believe that maybe they did do something terrible, causing their partner to feel hurt and then to treat them badly. Longlines begin to change their behavior and try harder in the relationship. The power of the victim erodes as their will weakens. They may even begin to doubt their own reasoning ability. Instead, the perpetrator gains strength and power in the relationship.

Faultlines are often gifted artists at making Longlines feel guilty and responsible for what they do. This is the way that they have survived in life, and for them, it was necessary. They have had to stay on top, taking control of the relationship by using the other person's good nature against them.

YOU GO DOWN—THEY GO UP

Do you ever feel responsible for the bad things your partner does? Faultlines will rarely take responsibility, although they sometimes pretend to in words that they do not mean. Most often they, shamelessly, put all the blame on you. Faultlines blame other people for what they do and what happens because of it. Faultlines needs to look good in public.

Bottomlines just do not care.

The experienced Longline will quickly get out of a new developing relationship that hints of this kind of potential emotional or *physical abuse*. Seasoned Longlines recognize the escalating frequency and intensity of the undulations of an *abusive relationship* and wisely bolt out the door. This, in turn, forces the people with Faultlines and the Bottomlines to reach for younger, more innocent and trusting partners. They may claim the attraction is to a "hard body," but it is really to someone with a lack of defenses. The young novice Longlines typically have absolutely no real-world experience, no education in adult relationships and no protection from a calculated seduction. Taken to the cleaners the first time around, these innocents incur damage emotionally, financially, and physically.

If people with Faultlines are this bad, why do people fall for them?

Here is the catch: People with Faultlines, like Bottomlines, are always more exciting, erratic, unexpected, like the first time on a roller coaster ride, exhilarating for a while. Because of the high, then low, then high, pattern, they become not only thrilling, but also *addictive,* even though the thrill is not worth the insanity and pain they bring to a Longline. Remember, the abuse is often unstoppable, and unless you shut down emotionally like them, this relationship may destroy your happiness.

A good Matchline relationship feels like the slow chug of the "Little Engine That Could." A badly matched relationship with a toxic partner is chaotic and rapidly changing. Constant and sure love will rarely develop in Bottomlines or someone with a Faultline, unless they commit to serious change for themselves. You will end up doing all the giving, while they do all the taking. They are rough rides. Nevertheless, they will always *appear* hotter and more exciting than a steady Longline "boring, freight train" lover can.

LOVING THE PERSON WITH A FAULTLINE

Everyone defines trauma differently. If someone molested, severely neglected or abused you, then your Line may be compressed or even cracked and faulted. A good, healthy relationship becomes more possible when you and your partner understand the impact of trauma and its effect on your ability to trust and to give. You can choose to guard your relationship from reactionary lashing out or shutting down if you keep the trauma unburied, exposed to light, well discussed and eventually, accepted without shame. This may require the assistance of a good therapist, and it is a smart and a healthy option for you to make in your life.

The partner with a Faultline really needs empathy and understanding. However, it is extremely unwise if you are a Skyline to get emotionally involved or marry this person unless you are prepared to have a rough time, even trying to make it through a single holiday or any stressful time. If you choose to stay with someone who has a Faultline, you need to learn to re-frame the barrage of insults that Faultlines are likely to shoot at you. You must remain steadfast against his or her attempts to improve you, or remake you in a Faultline's image. You must hold your ground. A Faultline will attempt to love you as cruelly as his or her parents probably loved them. He or she knows no other way.

The result is that the Faultline's issues create a distance between the two of you. Sometimes this painful distance helps a Longline survive the relationship, but it is oppressive to your happiness. Do not try to change yourself in order to be loved by someone with a Faultline. You must steadfastly hold your ground. Your changing will not improve the relationship. Instead, consider focusing on your own goals for yourself.

Consider this: Would you make a person with a Faultline the person in charge of your lifeboat? Never! Faultlines must never be in charge of your children, your children's discipline or your life. Faultlines cannot be the leaders in a relationship. They are too confused about what is right, wrong and fair, and they may lash out cruelly at you or your children. The longer Lines must always lead the relationship. You cannot be subservient to someone that you suspect is mentally ill, no matter what familial customs or religious orders dictate. It is dangerous to do so.

You have an obligation to yourself not to ever settle for less than you deserve, or to ever consent to take abuse. No one should wake up in the morning hoping the day will be over quickly. Life is meant to be savored. Indeed, bask in your day and enjoy every moment possible. If you cannot do that in the presence of your partner, then you probably have the wrong partner. If you decide that you do, then insist that the relationship change, and let your partner know that if he or she refuses, you are left little other choice except to get out of the relationship. True Bottomlines and those suffering from dysfunctional personalities, severe untreated "Faultlines," along with unchecked alcoholics and addicts really need to get professional help to heal themselves and restore their capacity to love, because without treatment they only tend to hurt the ones they love.

CONTENTMENT AND PEACE

Sometimes we make desperate, self-destructive selections because we are afraid that we might never find another love. In some people's minds, loneliness is a fate worse than a bad relationship. Yet, finding true love is as wonderful when you are sixty as it was when you were fifteen. Do not be afraid to hold out for the real thing. Yes, it takes courage. When you find true love, it will continue to give you happiness all your life. If it is real, it will feel peaceful most of the time.

Above all, make sure your *mental health* survives your love choices. Admittedly, a good match with two Longlines feels boring at first, especially if you have been choosing people with short or broken Lines in the past. There may not be the stunning highs and lows of a dysfunctional love when you are with a good match.

If you are a Longline, then take the time to let relationships with other Longlines grow on you. It could just mean a lifetime of happiness.

Part 5

LINE LENGTHENING

"Where there is love there is life."

—Gandhi

Chapter 13
UPLINE: ADMIT TO CHANGE

*I*f you have never known true love, then stop *looking* for a relationship for now.

Instead, focus on making yourself a kinder human being, and happier and more content. See if you can lengthen your Line a bit to attract someone who is wise enough to value what you have to offer.

To maintain an ongoing relationship that is a bit of a mismatch, although still a good investment, begin work on small behavioral preferences that strengthen each of you as individuals, like health, safety, fairness, improving attitude, smiling, good-morning kisses and goodnight hugs. While early core belief and value systems are extremely difficult to alter, even with in-depth therapy, it is still effective to begin Line lengthening strategies in spite of such difficulties. Somewhere between the lines, you will find a workable relationship—and balance.

Take a thoughtful and systematic approach to your Line-lengthening. Qualities like **assertiveness, personal integrity** and **goal-setting** help to strengthen you and your partner, as well as the separate and all-important third entity: your relationship. As you both gain self-esteem and strong interpersonal skills, the relationship stability will automatically improve.

Conversely, you can expect little success if you attempt to change your partner in order to achieve balance in the relationship. Resistance, if not relationship failure, will result.

Personal growth that emphasizes techniques and behavior will help to balance a relationship. It is possible to have one or both partners severely lacking the attributes of a good match, yet the mix works and they manage to blend into a great synergistic relationship. However, situations like this are the exceptions. Most of us can stand a little tweaking and polish.

YOUR TURN

Working on you is all that you can control. Partners must make their own commitment to work on themselves.

If a partner refuses even to try, what does that say about his or her feelings for you? Maybe your partner is so inhibited and shy that holding a spotlight on his or her psyche is truly painful. Is it because he or she does not really care if you are happy or because your partner is overwhelmed in other areas of his or her life.

Sometimes you must be packing your bags before your partner chooses to pay attention. Unfortunately, that is often too late, as you may have already stopped loving them. Worst case, you must be prepared to leave a relationship that is genuinely cruel, toxically abusive or completely empty. Yet, if you have a well-meaning partner who is sincerely trying his or her best without making excuses, the relationship may be worth an additional investment of time while your partner struggles to improve. Meanwhile, focus on your own self-improvement. You will benefit from personal growth and be ready for a higher quality relationship with your current love if this relationship improves, or if necessary, you will be in good shape to move on.

If you must weed out toxically abusive people from your life, then you will need to be prepared and strong. Leaving someone you still love, but maybe are not in *love* with, is heart-ripping business, and never to be undertaken lightly or rashly.

SPARE CHANGE?

Can people really change?

As we have noted earlier, psychologists continually debate the influences of nature over nurture. Is it your DNA (nature) or your parent's and your decisions, (nurturing) that causes you trouble today? If it is your DNA, then you cannot change very much. Admittedly, a little hair dye, self-tanner, regular exercise, colored contacts and fancy shoes are simple changes we can make to adjust a few of the givens of our birthright. Nevertheless, how adults nurtured you from your earliest days of life shows as clearly to other people as the color of your eyes. The good news is that you can make adjustments in the emotional and behavioral departments also.

To start on that path, reduce the time you spend with truly toxically abusive people and seek out Longlines that want to nurture you.

YIKES, IT'S ME

What if you discover that you do not like your own Line picture?

If you have taken an honest look at your own Line (or your partner's) and it makes you cringe, there are opportunities to lengthen that Line. Sometimes great change occurs through circumstances. The big trauma of a heart attack, disaster or a car wreck can create tremendous priority changes in a person. Do you need a major tragedy to change yourself? There are many less dramatic and effective ways. Sometimes a distant, stoic dad finds a place in his heart for a grandchild and learns to love his wife better, too. Change can also happen when a person finds a true relationship with a loving God, a purpose or a cause.

However, of those who do choose to change and successfully do so, the secret is plain old hard work.

Unfortunately, the majority of people stay stuck in their mindsets and bad habits. Ask yourself how many bodies at the gym look as out of shape today as they did five years ago. Only a few sport the new and improved rock-hard abs. So goes the best intentions. That may be difficult to hear. Nevertheless, a relationship only needs one person to grow to help make it more balanced and healthy.

You may not achieve a total makeover, however, everyone can make tremendous improvements. If you are involved with a new Shortline and you are vacillating about breaking up or committing all the way, you will know soon enough if you need to move on. Once you are able to imagine your relationships in money investment terms—seeing it as an investment of your time, your money and youth—you will likely conclude that you cannot easily waste time in fruitless emotional-spending.

Are you still uncertain? If so, consider giving the current relationship opportunity to evolve once you have learned the concepts of Matchlines. The Quizzes on the Matchlines web site, www.drmollybarrow.com can reveal positive strengths of your relationship and any hidden pitfalls. Every step that you take toward your own self-actualization brings into sharp focus who you are and who you want to be. From that point, your future path will become crystal-clear.

Choosing your life-partner can affect your life more than your choice of college, house, doctor, or school for your children because your children's happiness, painful grief, and even your life are tied to it. You owe it to yourself to get it right.

Right now, this second, I can guarantee you that your current relationship will never be the same if you have the courage to begin a positive change. Seriously consider taking on yourself as a project, not your mate.

MOMMY DEAREST

Of course, it feels so much easier to focus on changing your partner. Unfortunately, all that effort is completely ineffective. It is wasted motion. Your interference in your partner's decisions is completely unappreciated and makes you his or her "parent." It is also a complete sexual turn off!

Choose to change only you. When you do, then **you force all the people around you to change, too.** There is no way to know in what direction they will change because that is a result of their decisions. If they change in a direction away from you, then you have garnered new information about your partner, and you will assess the benefits and costs of staying in the relationship.

Continue with your positive changes and see if your partner reverses direction. Nevertheless, you must stay on track to becoming all you can be.

If you lose a partner doing all the right things, then choose to believe that a better match, one that is right for you, will appear. The reward will considerably outdistance the loss.

HERE'S LOOKING AT YOU, KID

Do you need a **Line Stretch?**

If you are interested in relationship growth, with a little motivation, you can change from a relationship that is stifling, to the comfortable relaxed luxury of a better fit. Your Longline partner will very likely be eager to please you and will choose to make adjustments by backing away and meeting his or her needs sensibly elsewhere—that is when your partner comes to understand that this approach is what allows you to be comfortable in the relationship.

You can contribute to the overall quality of your relationships and maximize your own Line with dedicated self-improvement. By doing so, the relationship will naturally change. One partner can totally change the behavior and reactions of the entire relationship by taking action. When Fred changed his steps, Ginger changed her steps.

If you had a difficult childhood, substitute the constantly running negative "tapes" that were programmed into your head with more positive mental voices. See your doubts and hesitations as the enemy trying to thwart change. That is why you may need to avoid the people, habits, and places that keep you locked down into the same old patterns. Some people will not like it, and they will try to seduce you back into your old ways. Friends will exert their power over you, particularly when they are going in a negative direction themselves. They need you to be like them and to keep them company in order to validate and rationalize their own wrong directions and wrong choices. They also need an audience.

You do take on qualities and habits of your closest companions. Swans fly with swans. Bugs crawl with bugs. With whom do you surround yourself? You may have to make a difficult decision between two desires. However, determine what is healthiest for you and your family, because it will most likely be the right choice.

TURN OFF THE COMPRESSOR

The first step for Shortlines is the hardest of them all. Shortlines must eliminate or reduce their personal Line Compressors.

Systematically, Shortlines must choose to eliminate all of their addictions. If they do, their Lines will enjoy a good stretch, and their ability to love **will** wake up. The volume from the addiction nag in their head that calls them back to their poisons will get smaller and smaller. It will probably never disappear, however, it will get small enough to ignore. If they love their substances more than they love their partner, then they will only make excuses:

- "A few drinks are no big deal."

- "But I have to have butter-pecan ice cream every night."

- "My mate benefits when I indulge myself in porn."

Addictions that are left ignored tend to edge up on their own, not down. If you extrapolate the behavior illustrated by the quotes above into the future ten years from now, these same people will probably be having six drinks at night, be obese or have to work hard to feel aroused by a real person. Addicted people have to deal with cravings for bad habits left behind. Drugs, alcohol, addictive sex and various other compulsions create cycles of mental self-deprecation and failure, coupled with acquisition, physical pleasure and relief.

If addicted people choose to give it all up—for now—they will soon see how much better their relationship can be without extraneous activities that rob them of time, energy, money and interest that could go to their partner.

LOOK WHAT I FOUND!

Amazingly clean and sober, you and your partner will very likely begin to feel like kids again, happy, light and energetic. If you feel worse, you may have a little Faultline crack causing you some discomfort. Addiction is often useful to anesthetize painful events from the past. Therefore, if you struggle with coping when you are clean and sober, then you would benefit from a strong therapist to be there when you surface from the euphoria of your addictions, just in case you have been covering up a painful fault, or a past trauma that you are avoiding. You do not want to roll that memory log over to reveal lots of squirmy things all by yourself.

Without a blanket of addiction, you just might uncover a severe Faultline. The reality of deep painful memories may make you feel and behave even worse. You might want to go shopping for an experienced, supportive therapist. Rest assured that your therapist has heard it all before and will stand by you until you are feeling good again.

CLEAN AND SOBER

The remorse and amends are tough when you realize your addictions hurt other people, too. Alcoholics Anonymous, and several other organizations built on a 12-step program, really work—*if* you have the courage to walk in the door. You cannot do the serious work needed on your Faultline if you do not first lose your beloved/hated Line-compressor addictions.

You will benefit from professional help if someone molested, abused or abandoned you. If you were the molester, the abuser or the indifferent one, then you can get professional help, too. It may be very hard, but accept the fact that you had something unfortunate happen to you, and then work to reframe your current contribution to that trauma. By choosing to ignore the trauma, you are watering that weed every day. The good news is that you can clip its power by looking at it and talking about it with a good therapist.

When war veterans with their tough exteriors have come in for therapy, they remember being told to "just forget it," to repress their memories and go on with life. Most of their energy is required to smother memories and calm their anger and anxiety. Their families never have the whole person back again. We have to start from scratch in therapy and go through each tragic war memory before they are free to feel anything good again. We have a completely new crop of altered people from the Gulf Wars, who deserve paid extensive therapy before rejoining their neighborhoods. If you have experienced major stress, then recognize that it is better to get therapy as soon as you can to help you have a longer, happier future.

A GOOD SHRINK

Once you choose to "shrink" a trauma's importance, then the effect the trauma has on your behavior will diminish proportionately. You are obligated to reveal your Faultlines and Line-compressors to your partners, just as they are obligated to you to reveal theirs. Yes, all of them. Some partners may leave. Nevertheless, the start of peace and self-acceptance is waiting for you when you say, "No more will I be controlled and victimized by memories."

Once you eliminate the Line-compressors and deal with any Faultlines, then you are ready to have a better Line, healthier relationships and if necessary, you will attract a better new Matchline. Let us now begin this process by addressing the tough subjects.

MY PARENTS REALLY MESSED UP

Your parents' inadequate parenting is not about you. Yes, it impacted you, but assume that they did the best they could, with the training, mental health, intelligence, and patience that they had. If you were beaten, abused, neglected or ran away from home when you were twelve, that is a story. However, that story is not as much about you as it is about your parents. If any of these harsh things happened to you, then the adults in your life were inept at their job. They did not give enough protective care, and they failed to keep you safe.

Nevertheless, regardless of what happened to you as a child, you survived.

Now that fact is about you. Start there. If you can, forgive your parents' incompetence, great or small, not for their sake, but for yours. Repressed anger eats away at you physically and spiritually. Whatever hurt you, you can begin to seek therapy to repair all you can. Do not waste time hating your parents or yourself for the past. Worse, do not pretend that nothing bad happened while suppressing the memories and saying you had great parents. Yes, you may very well be emotionally restricted because of them; however, you are also here because of them, too. Acceptance without blaming is the hardest part of grief and a first step to healing.

At any age, you can find new people to be your family. Go out and search for Skyline elders who would sincerely love to parent you, value you, or simply have more to offer you than the dry well of your dysfunctional biological parents. Remember, Skylines want to redirect attention to relieve their own partners and your friendship could be just what they need to smother-love. No matter what happened in the past, you can give yourself permission to find a new Mom or Dad to love and let them love you.

Choosing to surround yourself with a new environment of love and respect can offer you a safe place to change, to learn how you act and react and to learn how you genuinely feel about yourself. Although you may not easily recapture the complete Longline person you could have been with appropriate childhood nurturing, if you are truly motivated, you can overcome many deficits.

WHO IS THE SHORTLINE?

WIFE: AGE 30, HOUSEWIFE

> I want more. I want more to the relationship than gray feelings. I feel drawn apart, and he just procrastinates. He has no close friends and does not seem to need anyone. He wants to go live on a houseboat. Well, I am not that adventurous. Imagine a toddler and an adolescent on a boat.
>
> We are just not in harmony anymore. He did not even remember

my birthday. I am so sad about it all.

I feel like my wedding ring is strangling me.

I never felt close to my mom. I am more close to my dad. I remember my dad holding my mom against the wall with his face red. It was an unpleasant household. No drinking, but definitely not fun. Dad was controlling, rigid, absent and yet, always the dictator. He is very successful, critical, and he scares me. Dad has been a recovering alcoholic since I was six.

My mom died in a car wreck when I was 16. I never got over it. I want to be cherished, to feel like I am in my husband's inner circle. I am silent, suffering in pain and he does not notice. Then I just blow up.

I am not going to drink anymore; I am turning out just like my dad.

HUSBAND: AGE 31, DENTIST

I am trying to diffuse all the anger we live with. She has put on weight and is not feeling good about herself. All the alcohol isn't helping her.

I have been telling little lies and I feel guilty.

My dad is Russian, stoic, solid. He does not respond, not to fear, not to happiness. He is an engineer.

My mom is a great Mom, does most of the work. She is educated.

I think I am working too much, and ready for a mid-life crisis. For about five years, the marriage has not had magic. I went on a weeklong ski trip. I came back feeling confused about my marriage.

My kids are great kids. I do not want to hurt anyone.

ANALYSIS:

This woman was behaving like a Faultline Doormat. She was also an incredibly genuine nice person when fear did not overtake her. Her anxiety and fear were driving her man away. She tried to be perfect and self-sacrificing, while she resented his freedom and carefree attitude.

She appeared in many ways to be a Skyline, however her losses and mistreatment created a fault on what might have been a very long Line.

He was the Longline only in comparison to her Faultline. She bravely began to work on herself and her relationship. She became more honest with herself and her husband lowered his expectations and demands of her. He learned to know her and judge her actions and reactions from her difficult past, not from his own experience.

She had to revisit age sixteen and grieve again for her mom, because in her father's household, her feelings were denied.

This couple was successful and salvaged a good marriage with pure love for each other, patience and hard work.

A CERTAIN DEADLINE

You are going to die. Sorry, but it is true.

Death is a rotten deal, and we all have to do it. Once you accept the limits of your lifespan, then you will have an increased motivation to make changes in your life now, rather than later. Choose to accept the fact that you are going to die too soon to accomplish all your life's goals. You have time limitations.

Try this: Imagine there is a brick wall. On one side, you are struggling with the concept of death, running from the truth. You cycle around like a hamster in a wheel, saying, "I don't want to die," and being angry at death. You get nowhere on your goals. Each day you do get closer to death.

On the other side of the brick wall is acceptance that you are going to die. A full color mind-expansion follows quickly thereafter. Maybe you have a plan for heaven or maybe you believe death is just the end. Only from this side of the wall does phenomenal and meaningful change begin in a person's life, after you finally deal with the concept of death.

If you think backwards, from death to now, what do you want the remainder of your life to be? Imagine yourself walking on the beach at the age of ninety-nine. What can you do today to help ensure the future you imagine? What do you want to have had your life represent? What rules govern your life that you embrace? What do you value about yourself and want to enhance?

If you can redefine your future—today—you can still have your ultimate life.

It is not too late to find redemption from your wayward ways and begin to live life in your style. Then, if you do have to explain anything you ever did, postmortem, you will have the right answers.

DREAMS

Do you have a dream?

Be aware that your friends and family may fear you changing because they might lose you as they now know you. They are deeply invested in your remaining the same, because many memories and relationships are based upon who you have been to them. Now, you have the audacity to want to change!

Your family may say the right words to your face; however, you just might have more resistance from them than your worst enemy. You know the subtle pressure, almost a mental lean on you by your family and closest friends, designed to push you back in place. That is okay. Just understand that they try to hold you back because they do not want to lose you. The more they adore you, the more they fear something bad might happen to you. Loved ones design these often-subconscious reactions in order to thwart changes.

Such road blockage is actually a misguided attempt to keep a relationship stable rather than a mean-spirited sabotage. Try to see their efforts as a form of love, and maybe in time, they will come to feel more confident about the changes you are going through. If you get angry with them, they may escalate their efforts to save, meaning block, you. You must persevere, because this is your one shot at life. Do what you want to do in spite of the opposition if you believe it is right for you. Did anyone else ever let you choose the direction of his or her life? Why would you let others dictate the direction of your life?

The exception occurs only if, in your lucid moments, you admit that you are really making a series of bad decisions. If you are abusing substances, then you are losing your senses. In that case, perhaps, you could benefit from some familial or best friend's advice. If they are trying to stop you from getting married too quickly, enlisting in the military just for the benefits, or investing everything you own in one deal, maybe take just a moment for a quick listen-up. If you agree that you are messing up your life, well then, that is different, your relatives may be right.

Otherwise, tally ho toward your heart's dreams. You must pursue your dreams or you numb down into a robot. Do you recall the moment that Don Quixote in *The Man of La Mancha* saw Dulcinea and came alive from his walking despair? Dreams keep you vital.

Are you too old, too feeble, or too "something?" Okay, you can still follow your dreams, just work within your limitations. Do you want to be a movie star? Land one commercial in Peoria and play a grandma, or go audition for community theatre. If you simply hand out playbills, at least you are in the action—the doing of life makes it great. Life is too short to be a cool observer or a bystander to the richness of the world.

Prepare to make a complete fool of yourself. Does a baby quit learning to walk because it falls two-hundred times? Failure does not matter. Failure is necessary in order to learn and achieve. Your opinion of yourself matters more than others' opinions of you. Do you like yourself when you quit, give up or worse yet, do not even play?

Just get in the game.

MINI MOMENTS

When do you celebrate your achievements? Choose to enjoy the process of the work, the dream of obtaining a distant goal. With each step, celebrate your progress. Do not wait until the job is finished to feel happy; be happy along the way.

You can make life a tragedy or a banquet by how you label the little moments. If you wait too long to celebrate, you might die or start to want a different goal. Take all the glory you can squeeze from an ordinary day and relish your moments before they are all over. Wear a tiara, or your dress shirt, and use the good china. Buy an Austin-Healy for your Sunday afternoon drives and wave like the Queen Mother. Why are you saving your cherished things for your kid's future garage sale?

COURAGEOUS ALONE

No one is going to applaud you for ordering water instead of vodka. No one will notice that you are thinking about taking a class instead of going to the mall again. If your goal is to lengthen your Line with self-knowledge, acceptance, education and perhaps therapy, in order to find or have relationships with longer Lines, you have to work hard. Mutual balanced beliefs nestled in a trust environment is extraordinary, but definitely achievable to everyone willing to make the effort. No one except you may ever acknowledge your efforts. Only you know how deeply down you started on this climb to a healthier, freer and happier self.

One great moment of unrecognized courage was when an agoraphobic patient (people so full of fear that they often hide in their closet) was able to sit through an entire movie in a darkened theater and not panic. Only she and I knew the courage that step required from her. We smiled big wide smiles together as she nearly burst with self-pride. Your triumphs are for you, not for recognition by others.

Have the guts to see where you are lying to yourself, or to others, and to recognize your negative patterns that are often obvious to everyone else. If you cannot see them, then you can hire a sharp therapist who will point out patterns without bias. Once you can see a pattern in your behavior, then all of your excuses fall flat. Then it becomes excruciatingly clear the next time you try to sabotage yourself. Just being aware can change mindless reactionary choices of pure habitual behavior into goal achieving success.

What is going to be important for you to have accomplished at the end of your life, when you are looking back reflecting on your life and nearly finished in this world?

Do you agree that prioritizing your health is very important, or you might not be around long?

Have you put away enough money over the years so that you can remain independent? Did you start working soon enough to satisfy the dreams that can only be satisfied when you are young and strong?

Have you followed your heart and conscience by doing the right thing so you are not plagued with guilt and remorse now?

Have you maintained a relationship with family members or (if they are unbearable) with your new adopted family-friends so that you are not left isolated in your last years?

If not, it is time to start a to-do list for the remainder of your life.

Life has taught us that love does not consist in gazing at each other, but in looking outward together in the same direction."

—Antoine De Saint-Exupery

Chapter 14
GOAL LINES

What do you value about your life? Are your values ambiguous? Hazy? What do you *really* want?

When you are rock solid in this area of your life, pervasive change happens.

Can you list your goals and values in a hierarchy of what is the most important? If you are spiritual, you may list your relationship with God first. On the other hand, perhaps you put family first. Did you include your health near the top? Without your health, you will not have much time to work on your other values and goals. How about integrity? Without integrity in both public and private actions, the direction you take will have little to do with a positive outcome.

Could you raise your self-esteem and stand for more by selecting different values? When you incorporate good values that are *your* preferences, you will be proud of yourself, and so will your partner. Right now, begin to stand for something great.

COMMITMENT

Can you commit to yourself, to your goals, your causes, and to the people you choose to love?

Commitment to yourself means that you work hardest for your dreams and goals, not everyone else's. Commitment starts in the morning and runs until you fall asleep. Your accomplishments reflect your commitment; because even with some bad luck along the way, committed people can become president or famous or happy. You can rarely attain big goals without commitment as a top value.

Commitment means that if you decide to lose five pounds or fifty, you don't take a few walks then give up; you work up to a walk of an hour or two each day until you succeed. Maybe that means you watch your calories and eat smaller portions of organic fresh food six times a day. Whatever it takes, you are committed. A nasty failure-voice that says you deserve a treat is not your friend. Commitment bears the pain and deserves the win.

The last stretch of your journey may require some reaching. Maybe you do not have complete confidence that you will ever succeed, but you get out there anyway and pound away at your goal. Eventually, one day, you are there. Significant change in the length of your Line is only possible with this kind of commitment. Do you admire people who commit to their goals? Can you commit to what you want and forget all the wavering, questioning and vacillating?

DISCIPLINE

Set your limits, tow the line—discipline.

Discipline is the making of good habits by doing them repeatedly, until it becomes second nature to run a four-minute mile, go to a Pilates class, or say no to abuse.

Weak parents who cannot teach rules and boundaries create aggressive, insecure children. Over-controlling, mean or sadistic parents create insecurity and sneakiness in their children. How do you parent yourself? Do you give in to that the cookie, coffee, drink, cigarette, wrong partner, over and over and then whine about it? The best definition of discipline is to **positively teach**, not punish or shame.

Teach yourself to succeed.

GRATITUDE

Be grateful to your parents for your life and your ability to think, move and reason. The decisions and sacrifices they made in their lives made it possible for you to know life. Perhaps that is all your parents could give to you.

As an adult, is it time to lose the grudges and bitterness for people who failed you in the past? A large majority of the people in your future will also disappoint you, betray you or hurt you, too. That comes with life. If you keep your mind on the failures of the past, then your world becomes about failure. Shine a dazzling smile into your life and let the negative go.

An excellent way to approach life is to start believing that you are lucky; that your life is bountiful. Be thankful for the opportunities and for the people who are coming into your life to love you. Maybe they are already here. You may find there is a short road to happiness when you choose to feel grateful. See what looking forward with hope and an attitude of gratitude can do to change your world.

CONTENTMENT

When you are in line at the bank, are you frustrated and impatient? Alternatively, are you standing in line really well, using the best posture you know? Are you completely ready to make the teller's day wonderful? Get it through your head that the mundane experiences of life happening right now *are your life*. Stop waiting for "I'll be happy when X, Y or Z happens."

Discontent is like a bad smell emanating from your facial expressions. Stuck in traffic? How could you use this moment? You can honk or make rude gestures, turn red in the face, and then die from excess cortisol very soon. Or, you can select a new CD while you idle, do some isometric exercises while you sit in the car, share a commiserate shoulder shrug and a smile with the pierced kid in the jacked-up compact car next to you. It is your call.

Responsibility

If you blame someone else, the world, your partner or God because you are not happy, then you will remain absolutely glued to your excuses and blaming. To get control of your own life means you stop whining and blaming others.

If you want things to be different, then you must be the one to do it. Other people are busy with their own lives. They will walk right over you and not even notice that you were waiting for someone to make you happy, to fix your pain or to balance your checkbook.

Repeat often, "I gladly take responsibility for changing my life."

Take your hits like a winner, make the best of a situation or leave it, then whistle while you work. What is the point of a defeated attitude that is mostly concerned with looking innocent? "I didn't do it." Would you want those words to be a synopsis of an entire irresponsible life? After today, be eager to say "I *did* it!" regarding your life decisions.

No one wants to come near a big baby, much less take the time to assist you in achieving your personal goals if you just sit there hoping for change. Do you feel powerless? You are powerful. The power to change is already in you. Choose to take responsibility for you, stand up, move forward and clean up any mess yourself.

Positive Attitude

A positive attitude is a lie. So is a negative attitude. Neither one is the absolute truth. However, positive attracts positive; therefore, that is the game to play.

A negative attitude is self-defeating, immature, and, frankly, *stupid,* because it creates a negative attitude in people that you may want to help you. Both attitudes are contagious. So which one do you want to spread around you?

If you are projecting resentment and frustration to everyone you meet because life is not going as planned, it is time to grow up and get your smile-face on. Life never goes as planned (deep down you already know that). How you bounce back is what is truly important.

You need to jump and dodge the obstacles of life until you start to get it right. If you naively expect a smooth run out of life, then frustration and disappointment will overwhelm you and keep you locked into the behavior of a two-year old.

Rather than be stuck in one place, you can grow in other directions until your Line is as healthy as possible. Then find a proper Matchline, or if already committed, try to fall back in love with your current partner. The whole relationship will be healthier because of the work you do on you, now.

Fake your positive attitude, even if you hate your life, because you will literally pull positive energy towards you from others. Eventually, you will feel positive for real and your life will change for the better.

TRUTH

In many health and popular magazines, there are clever articles about how to lie to your partner, how to deceive them, and when caught, what lies to tell. Do you endorse the mentality of: "Even though we are in this relationship, I'm going to sneak out the back door and say I didn't?"

Do you find it amusing when partners do not hold each other accountable for their half of the relationship? Why would a loving partner allow this? Does it take more strength to resist the desire of someone new for one partner than it does for the other? Women and men struggle with raging desire and passion, or excruciating boredom, equally. Sometimes it is for a stranger, a fantasy romance or the neighbor.

Temptation is no less difficult for a woman, yet often her punishment is worse. American society tolerates male indiscretion and weakness more easily, yet penalizes a woman with severe economic and judgmental consequences. Many religions declare that women tempt men to be bad and therefore, punish only her for indiscretions, too. Certainly, women did not write these rules for themselves.

Perhaps, we should hold men and women equally accountable for what they do in this deadly era of sexually transmitted disease. Unprotected sex can be a lethal weapon. Do you realize that if you have unprotected intercourse with an infected new lover, even once, you could not only die, but if you withhold properly warning your old partner before being sexual again, potentially also kill him or her? The stakes are much higher for experimentation these days. Deadly STD's have seriously curtailed the sexual revolution.

If you suspect your partner is unfaithful, then for your own health sake, you must require protection, always, or leave them. If you choose to stay in the relationship, then act on your own behalf and protect yourself from potential disease.

LINA AND PREJUDICE

Lina was a pretty, young woman married to a dominating, selfish, successful executive who was best friends with her equally dominating father, a proud doctor. She had long, gorgeous hair and perfect nails and the latest designer bag. She was also neglected, repressed and angry.

She had moved from her father's house to her husband's house, and they never had permitted her to make a decision for herself.

Her husband finally allowed her to take a part time job as an assistant at an attorney's office. She spent nearly every lunch hour at a motel with a young lawyer from the firm.

Lina said her husband was really much better in bed than her lover was. Why, then? Her lover was of a different race, and she did not use protection. She felt empowered by her infidelity that she said would make her prejudiced husband and father livid. She never told them, and they never caught on to her.

Her husband unwittingly played Russian roulette each time he reached for his wife due to her dangerous secret life.

ANALYSIS:

Lina was raised to be passive and submissive. She had no skills to be assertive or to gain real power in her life. She was so dominated that she became a Compressed Line to the low level of a Bottomline. She lashed out in a passive-aggressive assault on the health and dignity of her husband.

She perversely used prejudice as a weapon to even the score against her chauvinistic husband and father. Her actions were criminal against her husband and cruel to her lover.

Her husband, even with his many faults, deserved an opportunity to protect himself from exposure to disease from his wife and the other young man.

Lina savored each moment with her handsome lover, yet for all the wrong reasons. She achieved neither freedom nor a better relationship.

She was the ultimate loser.

VANITY

Too much time spent on physical appearance, hair, makeup or grooming will not bring you any closer to your life goals, and will rob you of precious little time you have to achieve what really matters to you. My appalled seven-year-old said with amazing clarity, "Makeup means you don't like who you really are," as I carefully applied my "face" for the mayor's Christmas party.

How much time do you spend preparing your hair or makeup, looking, hanging around and making yourself available, all for a relationship that remains elusive? Have you become obsessive about your appearance and more dependent on the approval of others? Such qualities eventually kill desire in the very people the big effort is meant to attract. Sometimes we concentrate so heavily on the preparation that we miss the race entirely. That same time spent in school, or working out or playing with friends and family has a higher payoff. Can you spontaneously play in a business suit, or high heels and artificial nails? On the other hand, do you just watch other people have fun?

As you refine your priority list, you may find that the time spent with superficial friends and making cool appearances at the right bars, wearing makeup and emotional masks, or time spent competing with the Joneses will be notably less important tomorrow. Maybe it is better to take that two-mile walk and concentrate on not drinking, smoking, eating or drugging your life away.

If you make your ultimate goal just to be married to a money-lifestyle, then you may obscure your ability to see the perfect Matchline standing right in front of you. Have you let your exterior matter more than you do?

A relationship based on artificial glitter is too fragile to last. Such a relationship is a burden that enslaves you to excessive grooming and spending your paycheck on hot heels or fancy shirts. Any new face can soon steal your partner if he or she does not love you for what rests beneath your attractive coating.

Use glitter only to attract, and then reveal the real.

INDULGE

If you are someone with a very long Line, consider focusing selfishly on you just a little. Try this with your partner's full support, if possible. If you are a big, soft giver all the time, then try not being so from time to time.

Longlines are in the mode of depleting themselves by perpetual giving. Are you giving to partners and children, and maybe aging parents all at once? If you were born anything other than a straight white male, then often you also give by allowing yourself to be intimidated or subservient in our society.

Some people give without limits to questionable organizations, churches or ministries, who confuse big business with finding a personal relationship with God or living spiritually. It is right and good to give in the ways that are important to you, but you are entitled to pleasures of your own, too. Find a balance to your giving and taking, or if you have no limits, the allotment of time, funds and energy can leave you drained.

If you are someone with a short Line or even a Bottomline, you probably do just fine in the "indulge-yourself" category. If you are the Shortline in your relationship, once in awhile try indulging your partner lavishly. It might not go smoothly at first because you are out of practice, nevertheless keep at it. Bottomlines, on the other hand, have no idea how to indulge their loved ones instead of just themselves. Maybe no one cared enough for them as kids to teach them. However, all Shortlines **can** become experts at giving happiness and pleasure to their partners. Such skills can be easily taught with help from their Longlines. Shortlines must fulfill their partner's fantasies the way their Longlines want them to at least some of the time.

TIMELINES

Set your goals with a timeline. A goal without a deadline is not a concrete goal that you intend to accomplish; it is just a hypothetical hope of something you would like to happen someday in the future. List all projects that are waiting for closure—everything that is causing you stress. Try to visualize when it might end, in days, weeks, months or years from now, and how serene your life might feel then. If you find you have unending stress, choose to change it now. Chronic stress or too much stress at one time will break your body down.

Learn to say no to other people's oh-so-urgent and unnecessary demands on your time. Guard the moments that are on your goal-achieving schedule, whether that's time to do your homework to get that degree you've always wanted, time spent gardening, or your hour at the gym.

I FEEL SO GUILTY

You may experience guilt for being successful or taking better care of yourself. Fight it.

Guilt is a tool used to keep people down and "in their place." Throw it away because it depletes energy, yet it does not change behavior or the past.

Can you achieve all that you dream? Others have. Why not you?

TRAIN LIKE SECRETARIAT

A racehorse cannot win a race on ordinary horse feed and training. Owners of million dollar thoroughbreds treat their horses as "special." Often because they are beloved, as well as moneymakers, owners take care of them like equine *prima donnas*. In fact, railway cars deliver grain rejected by the racehorse feed stores to breakfast cereal companies.

If you are expecting to run your races in life and finish near the top, then treat yourself "special" right now. You need the right fuel and exercise, mental attitude, stress reduction and safety. Do not wait for someone else to treat you right. Start treating yourself right and others will too.

If you are pushing yourself to the max, wrung out, running on empty, usually depressed, you may fall and break your legs. If you have children, elderly parents, or a handicapped spouse who depend on you and you go down, then so will they. So make the decision to indulge yourself, or else you are not likely to finish any races. You will break down on the "home stretch" when it gets the toughest. Conversely, the competition that eats right, exercises daily, gets regular massages, goes to a great therapist, and lives a peaceful life, will pass you by with accomplishments, leaving you coughing in their dust.

Realize that when you take great care of yourself, you are also providing for your dependants' survival. Rather than be trampled by the competition, or put out to pasture, take care of yourself first.

TIME ALLOTMENT

You need an overview plan, to be able to see your day as it unfolds, and organize it in small bits to accomplish your goals. Can you see your values and your goals reflected in your day?

Try this exercise: Draw a big circle on a page of paper with 24 equal "time slices" and put your current life activities in the sections. Eight hours of sleep is a big piece, yet without adequate sleep, you are not operating at full capacity. Maintenance of things that you already have, like going to the dry cleaners, car repair, dusting, and laundry, doesn't do much to help you progress. Did you include maintenance of you: hair appointments, manicures, doctors, exercise, preparation of meals and eating? Did you consider maintenance of others, children, pets or friends? Do these activities take up too much of your 24-hour time chart? If so, sell some of your unnecessary stuff. If you have nine pairs of black pants, could you sell seven? If you have a storage unit, time for a garage sale. If you find yourself hording "things" unnecessarily, calculate the wasted time, energy and money for the maintenance of unused objects. This may help you to pare down to minimum necessities.

Next, put in the money piece. How many hours do you spend earning money or contributing to the wage earner's ability to make the family paycheck?

You may find that available goal-achieving slices are slim-to-none. If so, then choose to make changes on your time chart that you can live with, and then include them in your life. Just for fun, have your partner draw your time chart and see if the two charts have any resemblance to each other. This is a wonderful way to communicate the stress of your obligations to an oblivious partner.

With this graphic depiction of your life in hand, it will be easier to ask, "What do I want to do today?" and compare the answer with what you actually did do all day. Clearly, if what you are doing is not in harmony with your life goals, then what are you wasting all your time doing? People have given up everything except their goal to scale a mountainside or cure a disease. Can you give up something, anything, to make room for your dreams?

Make the decision to develop a prioritized hierarchy of activities and tasks today. Add your personalized goals and values to the list, and then redraw your time chart. Schedule your new activities with a planner or calendar. You can keep refining it later. If you are disturbed with your time allotment results, you may discover a new path with effective time management and improve your success with goals.

Working on *you* will strengthen and bring stability to your current relationships. Best of all, doing this is going to feel great, as your efforts help to replenish your threadbare psyche.

*"We are not the same persons this year as last;
nor are those we love. It is a happy chance if we,
changing, continue to love a changed person."*

—W. Somerset Maugham

Chapter 15

DOWNED-LINE: OUTTA SERVICE

As you make changes in yourself, does your relationship seem too empty to endure? If so, have you made the difficult decision to leave the relationship, yet, are feeling scared? Worse, are you paralyzed by fear? Have you become a victim of your own dysfunction, abused not by your partner, but by your own dependent weakness?

Whether you realize it or not, you have the power to be in or out of a bad relationship. You may be held hostage by your insecurities and needs for this relationship right now, but you can learn to survive on your own.

Three changes can empower you and help to set you free:

- Get Familiar with You

- A Positive Life Coach

- Downtime and Spirituality

YOU TALKING TO ME?

In the previous chapter, we looked at many areas where you have the opportunity to get to know yourself better, become familiar with your real needs and effect many beneficial positive changes. You have taken a strong step in discovering who you are by learning Matchlines Analysis. The second of these changes that can richly empower you, is a **Positive Life Coach.**

Everyone has made tons of mistakes in his or her past. Early efforts with life's opportunities are often clumsy learning experiences. If the parent emphasizes and recounts the number of times the child falls down, fails to obey or struggles, then the parent hampers learning, and the child becomes full of anxiety. Add punishment to shaming and over-correcting the child for his or her little imperfections, and you will have all the ingredients to make a Faultline. Each new task is like learning to walk. You do not start out proficient. Becoming better requires failure, lots of failure.

If only those insensitive parents could be trained!

Imagine that you are a positive coach training a puppy or teaching a small child a new skill. You would require discipline and a good effort, while ignoring failures, eliminating all forms of shame, disallowing excuses, and boldly celebrating tiny fractions of success.

This is the difference between bad parenting that uses shame to control and humiliate versus good parenting that uses positive teaching and reward. When a child masters a task, the parent no longer needs to do that for the child. A parent who still ties a school-aged child's shoes is doing so because that parent needs to smother.

Age-appropriate expectations and limits encourage children. Children are born with the desire to achieve and master difficult skills if the learning process includes opportunity for failures. The opposite treatment creates broken-spirited children with Faultlines.

Most likely, your parents socialized you intensely for at least a decade. Your conscience gradually takes over this socialization job, which continues to modify your behavior along with input from society, environment and experience.

Do you now have a good parent or a bad parent conscience?

Imperative to your growth and future is to **get rid of the bad parent.** The goal is to turn the voice in your head into a good parent by replacing negative inner-voice tapes of the past with your new Positive Life Coach voice.

Why, you ask? The answer is because positive "brainwashing" is the most successful path to change with the least effort and fewest potential side effects. It really works.

DOWNTIME

Can you do Downtime?

Downtime is time alone without a partner, just time with you. When you are comfortable all by yourself, you gain personal power and freedom.

Learning to do the Downtime between valid relationships eliminates desperate, energy-wasting pseudo-relationships with unavailable or incapable partners. The individual who is comfortable alone creates a strong base. You can fill Downtime with Line-lengthening behaviors to increase the numbers and quality of potential partners, as well as to enhance your current lifestyle.

Learning how to do Downtime is empowering. Desperation and fear of abandonment may cause you to cling to a current partner, simply because you are afraid to be alone and lonely. Overt dependence is ice water on a new love's passion. You soon begin to smell like a dead-fish albatross around your partner's neck. You have to learn how to live alone before you can successfully be one-half of a couple. Many people never learn how to do this. They live with their parents, go straight to college to live with roommates, or get married right away to their childhood sweetheart. Some get apartments and first jobs, and then move a boyfriend or girlfriend in as soon as possible.

Even if they are sick of their partners and want to get rid of the relationships, they cling on desperately, lest the find themselves alone. When faced with a death or a divorce later, they panic. It is essential that you spend a period of your life, six-months (or a year if you are younger) perhaps, right after college, or in-between marriages or relationships just learning to live alone well.

Living alone does not mean you take every single opportunity to go to bars in hopes of meeting a lover to fill the painful, lonely void. Most of our mistakes in love result from an impulsive rush into promising deals, without taking some time to think things through properly.

Living alone means waking up in the morning and asking, "What would I like to do this morning?" or "What would be fun for me to do?" These activities do not have to include a partner. Ironically, Matchlines seem to come along as soon as you aren't looking and are involved in interesting activities, because you act self-sufficient—and that is very attractive.

I LOVE ME

Do you enjoy yourself?

Making yourself happy is a learned behavior. Until the time when you can wake-up in the morning, look at the day ahead, and excitedly fill it with activities that you want and need to do to achieve your goals and fulfill your responsibilities, you are still too dependent on other people. Choosing to take action will enrich you. Waiting for someone to do it for you will deplete you.

Planning a day alone and keeping a positive attitude can be a challenge. Accomplishing the feat of enjoying your own company opens up incredible experiences. Sometimes you will feel satisfaction for only a few minutes at first. Nevertheless, in time, your skill with personal time will grow.

Downtime has synergistic effects in all the areas of your life. Your self-confidence especially will skyrocket. When you learn to take pure pleasure from activities that you can do alone, you are unencumbered. The activity may include other people, just do not desperately require the presence of company to baby-sit you.

For example, it may be more fun to take horseback riding lessons with a friend, but are you frantically calling friends to see if they will take a horseback riding lesson with you? You take your $35 and go take a horseback riding lesson. In the middle of this fun activity, you may not even remember that you are, in fact, alone.

RESPECT SOLITUDE

Would you rather starve than go into a restaurant and eat alone? Alternatively, is it sheer pleasure to be waited on and to select from the menu anything you want without worrying what someone else might think, that it is too expensive, or has too many calories? Learn to indulge and to treat yourself as if you are royalty.

People who work in the helping community where they give all day, like therapists, doctors and teachers, often want to be alone. They do not want to talk to anyone or hear problems anymore. They want to have their personal thoughts, to dream a bit, maybe for the first time all day. They are creating ideas and they know time alone is valuable. You may think people are wondering why you cannot find anyone to join you for dinner. Instead, imagine that you look like a thoughtful, independent professional—not the dateless wonder that you imagine you are and that makes you cringe.

Once you have learned to do Downtime, you will never be a victim to your own fears. You are capable of walking away from a lousy partner and an abusive relationship. If someone is ever physically or verbally abusive, you know you can walk away and survive. You have been alone before and there is no need to stay in a relationship out of fear of living alone or the specter of loneliness.

Downtime helps you to handle threats of abandonment or unfair deal-breaking behavior in a relationship. "Unless you 'jump through this hoop,' I'm going to leave you!" and your answer to that can become a confident, "Here's your keys."

You will not be afraid. You will be able to say simply, "I need to live my way. If that is not possible for you, then you will need to leave. I want a partner in my life who treats me great. I will not have a partner who abuses me, otherwise, this is goodbye."

The right Matchline for you is worth waiting for, or working hard to achieve with Matchline Balancing if you are in an existing relationship. The wrong match will be toxic to all areas of your life.

If you never learn to enjoy Downtime, you will give in too easily. Your partner will do whatever he or she wants to do and you will be powerless to stop it. If your partner says that he or she is controlling all the money or any other unfair demand, you have to say "Okay," because you cannot imagine life without his or her security. If your partner is having an affair, you look the other way because you are afraid to walk out the door and be alone.

Until you are capable of losing this type of person (your man, your woman, your boss, your child or your parent), you are powerless in the relationship.

The alternative to this misery is that you will have to grieve for a time. Yes, it will be extremely painful, and yes, you will grieve several months, a year, maybe two or more, nevertheless you have the power to leave anyone who is abusive and start a new relationship, job or life.

Someone with high self-esteem would never want a dependent, cling-on partner who could not handle a little Downtime. Instead of feeling passion for them, even a Longline will feel revulsion and feel stifled by dependent weakness.

Why let yourself remain hobbled at the starting gate of a relationship when you could be riding a champion thoroughbred of Downtime courage? Try it! Great self-esteem and satisfaction will surface from knowing that you can do Downtime.

FINDING SPIRITUALITY

Being alone also provides you with an opportunity to work on your own spirituality. Without some deep thinking in this area, you are on automatic pilot. Whether you realize it or not, you already have some type of a belief system created by other people when you were a child; we all do. It is at the core of every decision we make.

Childhood superstitions, parental lectures, religious organizations and groups, media and friends all contribute to what you may just accept as "the gospel"—your version of right and wrong. Would you be smart to question everything before you make it yours? Without making the decision to do this important work, you will never know whom you really are. Without knowing your true spiritual self, you will forever shortchange your partner by offering only a partial package in a relationship.

Genuine spirituality does not have to depend upon religious rituals that serve to create guilt and to foster competition between people. Religious barriers between people (like the kind that say: if you do not belong to this "club" then you will not have after-life or receive special benefits) continue to divide neighbors and entire countries. For now, try to look deeply into your being to define your relationship to God, or to the universe, or what you believe in when you are introspective and alone.

Spirituality does not need a religious label or an instruction manual of prescribed dogma. Stripped of territorial parameters, what is your purpose in life? What do you want to accomplish on this earth? What is right? What kind of sin makes you recoil? What is your driving force, and what will finally fulfill you? Until you learn to get in touch with your spirituality and the answer to, "Why was I born?" then you will find yourself bobbing in a sea of confusion.

Whatever your answer is to your personal purpose in life, no one else can conclusively prove it, disprove it or use it to influence the next person's mind that is locked into a different belief system.

After you examine your spirituality and beliefs, then see if you can find and, if you wish, select like-minded people to join you in positive work, not just worship. Be cautious because religious fakes can sometimes be manipulative or have Faultlines no matter how often they quote holy books or attend services. Until you connect to your own spirituality, your desires and fears lead your behavior with little consideration for the meanings and consequences of those actions.

When you are one with your own spirituality, then you can be confident of what is wrong or right for you. You can think clearly, decide what is best for you, your children and the pet, and, if you have to, can even summon the courage to walk away from a bad relationship without even a glance back over your shoulder.

STAY OR GO?

A technique that may help you decide more clearly, whether to stay in a relationship or to leave is to ask yourself repeatedly, "If this person were not in my life, how would I spend the next few minutes, or the next few hours? How would I raise the children differently? Would I have a different job? Would I have a different kind of environment?"

As often as possible, choose to live your lifestyle in a positive, relationship-enhancing manner. Try to do things the way you would do if that person were not negatively affecting your decisions, if your partner was not in your life. In a healthy relationship, couples approach conflict, tragedy, morals, values, children and finances in similar, unselfish ways. If you follow your own heart, your own needs and your own desires, then a well-matched partner will have little conflict with your personal growth.

All relationships have some conflict because of the differences between individuals. If there is such a big difference that you find yourself unable to be you, to laugh out loud, dance when you want to dance, or take the children to a movie when you want to, then you might already be in trouble. If freedoms seem to be shrinking, then the Line Gap is potentially too large between two Lines.

In a good Matchline relationship, there may be frequent minor disagreements; however, the only things that cause painful conflict are substantial crises and very large problems. In a poorly matched couple everything is a crisis, every decision from what you have for dinner, to how to do the laundry, to how to treat the dog, is a crisis. This is usually the result of bad parenting, bad childhoods, addictions or untreated mental illness. If that is your situation, perhaps you need to consider eliminating these toxic relationships from your life, or at the very least, the two of you need extensive help handling conflict resolution.

BOUNDARY LINES

The wealth jointly owned in a relationship must be divided equitably or else resentment will begin to divide the relationship. Are you living in a one-sided dictatorship—with a king or queen who is sovereign and owns all, surrounded by his or her dependent loyal subjects—or is the family dollar divided into equitable ways representative of your needs as well as your partner's?

Some people think of money as an extension of themselves. Some use money as a means to control others. If you give up control of all the family money decisions to your partner, then he or she is the boss and you are the secretary. When you offer one partner a position of entitlement and power, it inevitably goes to his or her head. Soon the inequity of the rules in your relationship will spread pervasively throughout and make your partner feel that he or she has a right to do whatever "the boss" wants to while you wait at home by the phone. You *gave* up your power and started this downslide. This is the wrong position for you—if you want to protect and keep this relationship away from predators.

If one partner is consistently subordinating his or her needs to fit the other's, then that is an example of a Longline bending over into a Shortline's face. If your partner is acting withdrawn, then you know that it is mandatory that you do not give in to your partner today. Perhaps it is a great day to do something that you enjoy instead. Otherwise, imagine your resentful, hateful little face after a few hours.

If you are a Longline, then sometimes you score more points with a Shortline by being absent than by being present. Mean, resentful, or jealous emotions show clearly in your body language. If you act dependent and subservient, even a loving partner will curve away from you just to get breathing room.

Straighten up and expect equity. You will like yourself so much more.

KNOW YOUR STYLE

We each have different patterns of work. Some people have momentary flashes of brilliance, and then they go blank for a while—consider them Thoroughbred racehorses. Some people have steady, consistent medium levels of output—consider them Morgan workhorses. Some people appear to be stubbornly standing still while they invent new ideas, call them Einstein-like mules. Some people create in their dreams or while sailing on a sailboat. Some people work frantically for hours at an office and accomplish little.

You need to know what kind of worker you are, and be content to work within your own style, in your own comfort zone. Become immune to criticism from other people who have different work styles.

One of the advantages of self-employment is that you are able to be more of who you are by working within your own rhythms. Our patterns of work reflect the plethora of intelligence we have. Some people are smart with time units. Some people are smart with logic. Some people could never maneuver in New York City, yet know the weather from smelling the breeze. Everyone is talented and smart enough in his or her unique way.

If you are trying to be a nine-to-five person and you are built for flash speed, then you are squeezing into work shoes that do not fit. You need to "Blacksmith" yourself into comfortable shoes and do your style of work.

YOU CAN LEAVE YOUR HAT ON

Do you feel ashamed or frustrated because you do not currently have a successful relationship, and a great job, and a new house, and many friends?

Social pressures once defined a woman in terms of her relationship and defined men in terms of their employment. Society also pressured women to be chaste and men to seek multiple relationships, encouraging images of a playboy over a family man. Consequently, many men and women found their "designated roles" to fail to provide the glossy promises of happiness portrayed. Question who is defining the behavior within all rigidly designated roles.

Most men and women naturally want the closeness of a family and good relationships. They also want to be successful at their vocation and free to pursue their dreams. Usually, a conflict in designated roles ensues. Mother vs. Entrepreneur? Father vs. Husband? Good Daughter vs. Girlfriend? Devout Member of the Faithful vs. Party-Animal? Executive vs. Boyfriend?

How many hats do you wear? Is everyone really supposed to have it all, great job, great family, great looks, and great life? Residual role expectations can leave you exhausted.

Find the hat that fits you best, and wear it proudly.

DADDY'S GIRL

Virginia's Dad had his own idea of who she was: his little girl. He loved her with expectations that he based on his inflated opinion and idealistic image of Virginia. Unfortunately, Dad was operating with some misinformation, a lot of omissions, some truth and his own positive prejudice.

Dad did not know the real Virginia.

Dad knew and adored a confectionary version of his daughter. His vision of his daughter made him happy until Virginia did something normal for her and very disappointing for him. Then Virginia felt guilty for not living up to her Dad's made-up version of herself.

Virginia was used to basking in Dad's adoration, but when she disappointed him, it hurt them both. Virginia loved her father, and knew that her actions hurt him. Her Dad's love was simultaneously both wonderful and claustrophobic.

Virginia knew she was the Shortline in her relationship with her father. Sometimes she just had to get away so she could be herself. She feared losing his gracious love because he could make her feel wonderful. She passively let his idea of her rule their relationship. She became more astute at hiding large portions of her life, like wild fun times, pot smoking, biker blues bars, and anything else that might cause him to reject her.

Virginia considered her Dad to be her best friend, yet she could not share the good or the rotten adult experiences with him anymore. He wanted to keep her a little princess, even though she was all grown up.

In order to be free to be herself, Virginia had to shut her Longline dad out of major parts of her life. They drifted apart, and Virginia stopped calling him except for holidays. Virginia vowed when she was older to accept as many of her own children's idiosyncrasies as she could to avoid driving them away.

Virginia's Dad never figured out that by putting Virginia on a pedestal, he forced her to leave him. If Virginia had assertively taught her father who she really was, she might have had less adoration, however maybe she would still have her best friend.

Sometimes societal pressures push you into desperately settling for any relationship just to fulfill the role. Loss of self-esteem is just one of the severe consequences resulting from succumbing to predetermined societal roles or familial roles.

Individuality Is Cool

Take the forced hats off.

You and you alone need to decide if you must wear high heels or a tie to be good enough to do your work. You decide if it is right to be poor in money and rich in time. Dreadlocks are just a hairdo and lapel pins are simply adornment, not indicators of a person's true character. Whatever is different about you, you must voice your opinion and have a "say." Because each time you do, the prison door opens a little more for oppressed people everywhere.

You need to decide if it is right to invite your "Ex" and your current partner to the same holiday party. Try it. It *might* work and if it does, your children will love having both of their parents around at the same time. You decide if you leave work to attend your kid's ball game, even if it costs a half-day's pay. Learn to negotiate these rights and be proud to be different from the status quo.

A society collapses when it becomes too generic and constrained. Individuality makes the entire system stronger. Strict conformity always implodes into chaos. You have the right to be considered "weird," which usually means being a little bit different from the next person—not necessarily being weird for weird's sake, or to seek attention.

Try to avoid deliberately stepping on anyone else's toes or attempting to convert them to your own form of weirdness. Let them be who they are—unless by virtue of your good example they want to be more like you, and then if asked, help them to understand your values and perspectives. Allow yourself to be unique; or better yet, celebrate your own inherent uniqueness in all the ways that make you happy.

To have freedom of speech, to have a unique religion or non-religion, to have a traditional or nontraditional family, to work for a big company or your own small business, to be involved in your community or to live on a mountain top, as well as the sacred right to be a little weird, are all hard-earned constitutional rights. How many people gave their sons and daughters lives, or their own, to protect these rights?

Vigilantly protect your right to be different, in your family and your community, and protect the rights of everyone else to be peacefully different, too. Before the "real you" gets too lost in what everyone else tells you that you should be, become a rebel *with* a cause. There is only one spectacular you.

Part 5

LINES OF COMMUNICATION

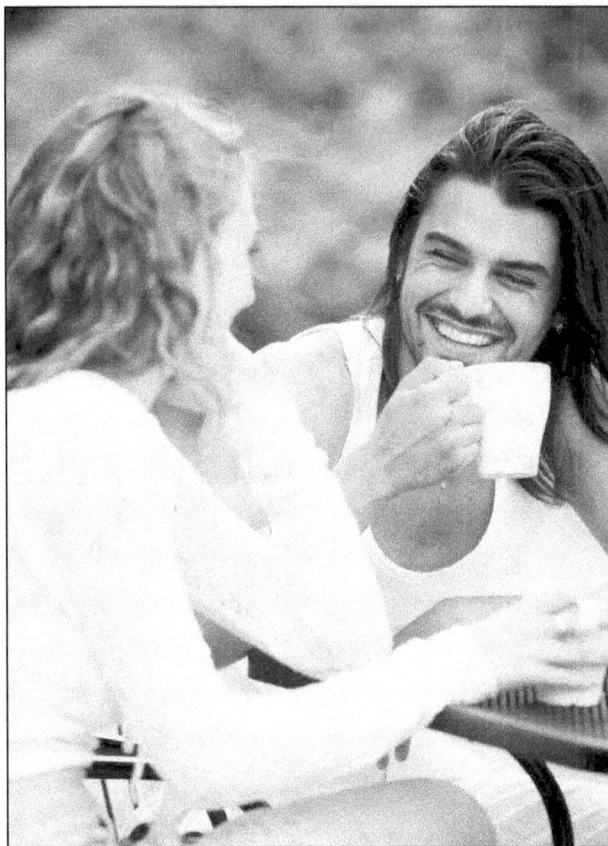

"Time is too slow for those who wait, too swift for those who fear, too long for those who grieve, too short for those who rejoice, but for those who love, time is eternity."

—Henry Van Dyke

Chapter 16
RECEIVING LINE

The first step in any healthy relationship is open and honest communication, which is essentially the exchange of information. As social creatures, it is vital to our existence. That is why we watch television, read books, newspapers and magazines, surf on the Internet, write letters, chat on the telephone and visit our neighbors. Achieving clear communication is something we unconsciously work on every day.

CROSSED LINES

Shortline says to Longline: *"My best friend growing up was my dog."*

Longline hears: *"Aw, he must be a kind person if he loves animals so much."*

Shortline means: *"I had such a lonely childhood, with an absent father and a depressed, withdrawn mother, that my only friend was the dog."*

WHISPER IN MY EAR

When interacting with people around you, the three key communication components that occur as you give and receive information are: 1) **Intake, 2) Processing and 3) Responding.**

INTAKE

Successful intake is the result of skilled **listening.** You cannot listen to another person if you are simultaneously formulating a comeback. If you can imagine tossing an "idea ball" back and forth slowly between two friends, a slam-dunk into someone's face has no place in a conversation, negotiation or discussion.

People who want growth in their relationship must reduce communication to taking turns respectfully, at a very slow pace or it becomes a fight. Good communication may require hours or days of processing the information between the steps of listening and the last step of responding. If you are struggling to communicate, you must slow down to a verbal crawl and restrict any interruptions.

Begin intake with one partner speaking, the other is only to receive, relax and listen. Only one partner has the floor as he or she speaks about a subject for five minutes or less. The speaker uses short simple statements that start with **I** (never **You**).

The receiving partner listens quietly until the end of the short speech, and then restates the other's words without any of the sarcasm, grunts or faces that usually accompany a highly conflicted discussion. Restate your partner's position honestly and fairly. No matter how OUTRAGEOUS the words may seem, no one gets to react to them. You only get to listen to your partner expressing their feelings. You are listening, not thinking.

Then, take a break. Do not react emotionally to the speaker. Take time to let your mind dominate the rush of emotion that may result from your partner's comments when you disagree.

After a while, it is your turn to have the floor, freely speaking your opinion for five minutes or less without interruption or corrections of any kind by the first partner. When finished, the receiver partner acknowledges the second partner's position as stated. If this process escalates, or starts a firing squad of sharp remarks, stop and cool off.

If emotions get a little heated, try holding hands gently while you take turns talking. This trick works on everyone, because it is so hard to be mean-spirited while gently holding someone's hand. If someone pulls a hand away defensively, you know to stop talking and wait until he or she "gets a grip" and can take your hand again. **Offer your hand,** rather than take his or her hand in an intimidating manner.

Processing

Thank each other for listening and acknowledging the other's point of view. Now stop talking about whatever the topic was and process the information by yourself, such as go take a walk, do some laundry, take a shower. Most conflict dissipates when a couple thoroughly listens to each other's opinions without interruption.

Take a whole day to process the information, if you can.

Responding

Remember that you love this person and someday you will probably share grandchildren together. Speak to each other as if you intend to spend the rest of your life as best friends. *Arguments* have a winner and a loser. *Conversations* have two winners. Make sure that you are discussing solutions in a respectful conversation rather than arguing.

Offer a compromise to solve the issue at hand and let your partner think about it. Give them time. Do not follow him or her from room to room, or he or she may turn on you like a cornered dog. Be sure that both partners offer a creative compromise of their own design.

This goal-directed give-and-take begins to resemble sitting in the showroom with the car salesperson making the deal. Go back and forth pleasantly and thoughtfully with offers until you two are pretty close to consensus. In the big picture, few topics are worth fighting about. If you are certain the best color is red, yet, your partner thinks the best color is blue, which one is correct? One hundred years from now, will this issue matter?

If one person gets an advantage this time, then perhaps in the next discussion the other partner gets the edge, as you learn to compromise. Successful relationships are not what you see dramatized on television. Fighting makes great soap opera moments, and awful real relationships. Calm down, rather than escalate, to save your relationships.

READ BETWEEN THE LINES

The art of communication—whether someone is trying to tell the whole truth or is blatantly trying to cover it up—requires a thoughtful approach with honed listening and response skills. Try to listen so closely and carefully that you hear what your partner does not say. Your partner sometimes reveals the truth by what he or she avoids mentioning.

For instance, your new date may say, "My mom raised me. She is a saint." You might deduce from that comment that your date is warm and loving and adores Mom. However, under that comment might be another unspoken statement: "Dad was not there." Was the father deceased, did he leave the family, was he a workaholic or an absentee alcoholic? Any or all of those answers could have caused substantial suffering—suffering that has shortened the Relationship Capacity Line, created a glitch, or even worse, a sometimes un-repairable break that makes a wonderful child an emotionally skewed adult.

CROSSED LINES

Longline says to Shortline: *"Does this dress make me look fat?"*

Longline means: *"I'm feeling insecure and would like you to reassure me that I'm still attractive to you."*

> **Shortline reacts: Needing to keep control over her, he lies and says,** *"Yes, you need to get on the treadmill."*

If you suspect the possibility of severe past trauma, you need to delve further by asking the right questions in an unobtrusive and sensitive manner. Information will slowly trickle out. You will not get every answer you seek overnight, so do not push too hard during initial conversations. You can always bring it up later in a different context. Just be certain to pursue the subject until you are completely satisfied, even if you cause a little irritation with your questioning. You have a right to know what you are getting into, and your partner has an obligation to tell you.

Would you buy a dress or business suit whose inner seams were unraveling, even if it looked fabulous on the outside? Would you buy a sports car with no clutch? Invest adequate time in "due diligence" to make a wise investment in your partner, too. Do not buy without inspecting the goods carefully. Whatever your partner is or is not talking about can be emotionally loaded for them. If trauma is affecting them internally, then later it will show up externally in the way that they treat you.

Knowing only the good side of your partner leaves you vulnerable to heartbreak, emotional and financial ruin, and your kids in therapy.

Whatever you do, do not ignore these clues or deny the truth and impact of them to yourself. If you do, it will haunt you later when you realize that all the signs of an emotional time bomb were there, but unfortunately, you made the decision just to look the other way.

At a minimum, satisfy yourself with this in-depth inquiry and resulting information to ensure that these relationship land mines *are not* there waiting to affect the relationship.

"Grow old with me the best is yet to be."

—Robert Browning

Chapter 17
STRETCH LINES

To find harmony in your relationship it is important to know the emotional buttons that lie within your partner silently waiting for you to press. If you have already committed to someone, then these techniques can help you know each other better. If you are not already in a committed relationship, and your goal is to find a healthy long-term love relationship, then you must politely investigate a potential partner.

Despite your initial feelings of thrill and excitement, and your own willingness to overlook the "little things" during the budding of a new relationship, your future depends on your investigative prowess. You must examine and compare the emotional heritage of your potential partner's family, with the way you remember your own life experiences. You must be willing to analyze family histories in order to benefit from Matchlines and to avoid potential future heartbreak.

Take the time to hold intimate and honest conversations early in the relationship. Full disclosure need not happen in one sitting. Conduct your information gathering conversationally, never like an inquisition. Simply ask your partner about his or her mom and dad, and be curious about your partner's early experiences in life younger than ten years old. Learn about a partner's history, behavior patterns and past before you ever consider sleeping, marrying or trusting him or her with your heart.

A potential partner rarely spontaneously heals from early trauma or bad parents. You could pay with tears and a broken heart if you choose a Line that is much too short for you—or even one that is too long for your own Line and the Lines remain unbalanced. The Line that matches your Relationship Capacity Line may have had some bad days in his or her life, may not have had stellar parents or the best relationship past. Even so, someone may be perfect for you if both Lines closely match. That is why it is essential to know your Line and your partner's.

Your investigation need not be a detective-styled interrogation. If you are too heavy-handed about learning about your potential partner, you may scare away the truth. Early in a new relationship, people often portray themselves as they wish others to see them by putting their best foot forward, not as they truly are. After you hear the first version of a statement, ask a second time, "What else is bothering you?" or "Is that all that happened?" This gives a person a second chance to tell the truth and is a most effective technique when you suspect you just heard a little lie or big omission.

Some partners may react in a hostile and defensive manner and accuse you of prying. Nevertheless, your future, your physical health (think HIV), or your finances could be trashed by choosing the wrong partner. Therefore, stand your ground and ask all the questions that you want over time as you get to know your partner better. Watch out for defensive reactions. If your questions trigger any sort of violent reaction, that is a big red flag.

Questions you might ask that will not make your potential partner think they are undergoing a background check or feel defensive may resemble the following questions:

- "Tell me about yourself? Where did you grow up?"

- "What does the word 'love' mean to you?"

- "What is your favorite childhood memory? Why?"

- "What do you remember most about your grandparents?"

- "What scared you most when you were a child?"

- "What did you get in trouble for as a kid?"

- "Did you like school?"

These are only a sampling of the endless questions you could ask a new friend, neighbor or lover in order to get to know him or her better. While some answers may end at a brick wall, others may open up important new areas of discussion. However, be careful. Some questions, asked with the most sincere of intentions may be met with anger by an extreme Shortline.

The **Singles Quiz** on the web site (www.drmollybarrow.com) will help you graph your Line and show you how to recognize a good match for you based on important questions about who you are. If you are in a committed relationship, the **Couples Quiz** will help reveal strengths and weaknesses of your current relationship and provide tools to make your relationship stronger and feel more comfortable for both partners.

LIE-ABILITY

When you begin this search for truth about someone else, you will undoubtedly face the dilemma that whatever someone tells you about his or her childhood, it is only one version—or perception—of the truth. As they say, "history" is never the simple facts, rather it is "stories" told by historians from their perspective—most often, the winners of wars, who get to decide how they want history to remember them. Any initial confessions you hear from a potential partner can be deeply sincere or completely untrustworthy as your potential mate tries to impress you, or perhaps lies to himself. It may only be what he or she has chosen to believe.

Nevertheless, getting to the truth is still the goal, even if you have to "read between the lines" of what someone told you, or compare information with your prospective partner's friends and relatives in the normal course of conversations.

When coping with emotional trauma, people tend to block out painful memories of their childhood. Layers of defenses and distorted memory bury the truth beneath them. Sometimes, other people in your partner's life when they were young, who had their own self-protective agenda, may have altered stories to cover an abused person's vivid childhood memories. Family members, who filtered the truth by denying incest, alcoholism or cruelty, may base these fabricated stories on lies, jealousy or distortions. Often when trouble occurs in a relationship, blaming the partner is the first line of defense for a very short Line.

Intimacy inadequacies are often imperceptible to the one who has them, just as symptoms of depression or mental illness are typically first observed by others, rather than by the individual having difficulty. The truth is not easy to find, but persevere for your future's sake.

CROSSED LINES

Longline says to Shortline: *"I can't wait to meet your father! When can we have him over for dinner?"*

Shortline hears: *"You want to entertain the man who neglected me, abused me and belittled me my whole life? Now I resent you, too."*

As honest as we believe that we are, and strive to be, we are also prone to humiliation, embarrassment, sadness and anger in certain situations. Emotional intensity distorts memory, especially about formative events that have a profound influence on our lives. If an event causes too much pain and anger, fabrications and lies may be emotionally necessary to mask and insulate the hurtful memory. Sometimes events are repressed and completely forgotten until triggered by an event.

How an event is labeled and remembered is sometimes more important psychologically than what really happened. The same event for two different children may be a trauma for one and uneventful for another. If a thief steals a child's bike and the child assumes that he will just get a new bike, then it is not a big deal. However, if a child feels violated by the thief, or a parent beats him or her for the loss, then it becomes a traumatic memory.

On the other hand, sometimes people minimize what really happened too much. Incest, alcoholism, rape, early sexual experimentation, abandonment, the deaths of loved ones, physical and verbal abuse, shame or humiliation—all of these are significant Line-shortening occurrences. Problems occur when, as adults, we deny traumatic memories, whitewashing our childhood. The trauma remains in the form of hidden glitches in our psyches, directly affecting our relationships.

Truth is evasive. Have a healthy skepticism while you are gathering information with respect to what you hear, and make sure you pay very close attention to behavior, as "actions *always* speak louder than words."

"If you would be loved, love and be lovable."

—Benjamin Franklin

Chapter 18
BODY LINES

*I*f you have done your relationship homework, then you will have studied the art of body language. You must rely on body language to tell you what is really happening inside people—despite what is said. Body language communicates the truth more consistently than words do. A laugh, a raised eyebrow or a grimace are unspoken responses that do not require words to communicate a message. They are quiet indicators of what is going on inside your partner. Sometimes, you speak with opposing meanings, too.

BODY LANGUAGE

Your words say one thing and your body language may say the opposite. **Believe the body language.** Body language reflects both positive and negative emotions, and is much closer to the truth than the "words" someone tells you.

We all react in these self-protective ways occasionally, so it is perfectly normal, and not always a means of intentional deception. The trick is to observe your partner's reactions linked with a subject that may be a glitch creator, like abuse, molestation or addictions. If, "I like to have a glass of wine with dinner," is accompanied by an eye spasm, then that may be a red flag on the subject of alcohol. If you ask, "Did your dad drink a lot?" and his or her legs quickly cross away from you, then that is another red flag.

Never ignore a body language red flag. The body moves in habitual patterns that you can memorize and read like a book. Soon you will recognize body-activity patterns when people are lying, exaggerating, or completely sincere. If you come across these responses as you delve into your new partner's past, then bingo, you have hit pay dirt. The timing of the shift in body position as someone talks about Aunt Lucy, or any subject, is crucial. If he or she is talking about what a great time summer camp was, and you spot the neck flush, then perhaps something else happened at camp—something that is protected and hidden that he or she may never volunteer to tell you.

After some time, and with a little practice, you will begin to understand how your partner reacts to certain situations. You will recognize a body pattern when he or she is amused, sincere, lying, or is just squirming away from an undesirable topic. If you are encountering body language associated with negative emotions, or you have encountered half-truths or unexplained holes in certain stories, focus on your own communication skills and try to coax out the truth.

Use body language clues proactively as a means of learning new information about your partner. You might casually mention other people, like their mom or dad or stepfather, and then watch for his or her body to close up protectively—that is, see if arms fold across a chest or legs cross away from you. If so, then subconsciously, he or she is telling you that you are now the source of a threatening question that makes you dangerous. Regardless, always keep in mind that your job is not to pry to make your partner uncomfortable or ashamed, rather to subtly uncover any emotional damage that might be there. Right now, see if you can become aware of what your partner's body says to you. More than words, our body language speaks the truth in the closest relationships. Only then can you make an educated decision about becoming more involved or intimate with this person.

BODY TRUTH

If we were to take a poll, we would probably conclude that the biggest problem we face at work, school, home, or in public is poor communication. You know you are having a problem when you find yourself saying:

- "You wanted it when?"

- "I told you I do not like that."

- "We agreed we'd meet an hour ago!"

- "Didn't we talk about this already?"

- "That's not what I ordered."

Frustration is often a symptom of poor communication. Try considering that you have a communication problem first, before you assume the world is out to get you. Achieving clear communication is something we unconsciously work on every day.

Fear is an important clue to hidden glitches. People who fear consequences will often lie to protect themselves. The act of lying creates more fear. Dishonest people are often fearful people, and if they have even a shred of a conscience, they worry about discovery or divine vengeance. A fearful body displays certain characteristics that you can observe. Imagine that you are a cave dweller and you see a tiger in your cave.

The following physical adaptations happen:

- Blood flow increases in the arms and legs and decreases everywhere else

- You feel faint

- The mind goes blank

- Digestion stops

- Elimination can be immediate

- The throat tightens, the jaw clenches

- Breathing becomes shallow

- Heartbeat races

- Cortisol rushes to every cell

Our bodies have not evolved much since our cave-dwelling days. Do you see why chronic fear and stress can do tremendous internal damage?

Scholars have an immense compilation of work on the subject of communication and body language. The following common reactions indicate stress, fear, discomfort and possible dishonesty. Watch for any physical changes occurring in your partner during discussions of important, stressful subjects.

- Neck flush, rosy rash appears on the neckline

- De-focused staring eyes, expressionless face, slack-jawed or teeth grinding

- The speaker will not look at you directly in the eyes, or will tend to look down or away at other objects while speaking, followed by a piercing stare to see if you caught them at their lie

- Long sighs or pauses

- Muscle tension: large, visible vertical veins in the forehead, the throat tightens so pitch changes, a high-pitched or inappropriate laugh

- Nervous motion: hands or feet in motion

- Closing up and away from you: body posture closes up to protect the vulnerable chest and belly, arms fold across the chest and legs cross away from you, shoulders shift away, head angles away protectively

- Dry mouth causes swallowing and lip licking

- Tightening lips, smiling strangely, eyes squinting

- Narrowing or dilating of pupils in the eyes, nostrils flared

- Nervousness, perspiration, scent, smell of fear that may even cause your pet to react

- Muscles twitch vertically, often eyes to cheek or cheek to neck

Study body language if you are tired of deceit. Read the truth as spoken through the body and behavior—never by words they say. If you ask someone if he or she is cheating on you, most will say no, hoping to avoid unpleasant confrontation. Even popular magazines coach people to deny everything—especially when caught! Some people may believe that their home and security might be at risk if they are caught cheating, so they lie. However, if their pupils narrow, their neck flushes, their legs and arms cross away from you and their lips tighten, perhaps you can ask them again. Even if your partner is adept at hiding dirty little secrets, few can deceive the trained eye of an observer schooled in body language.

Your job is to uncover emotional damage and deceit, hopefully **before** you commit, not after you have a mortgage and three kids together.

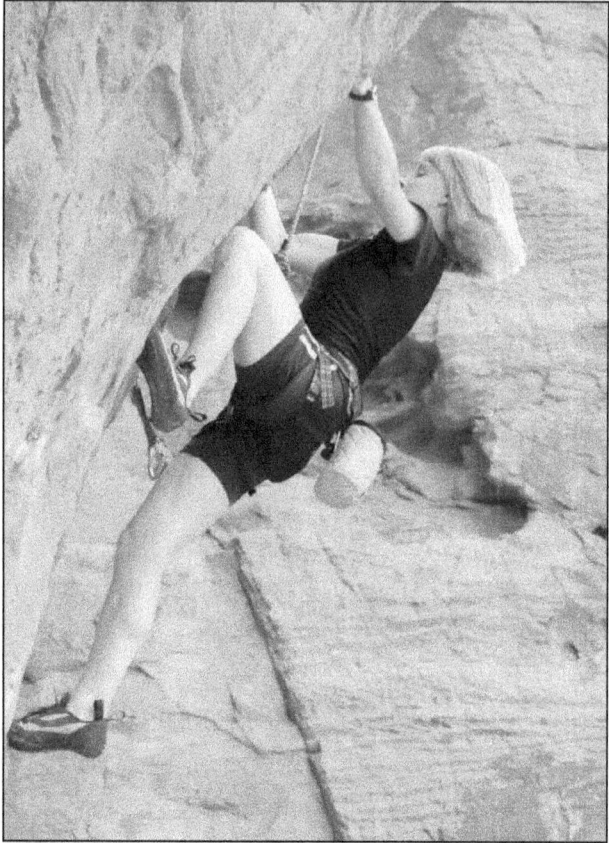

"*Love is shown in your deeds, not in your words.*"

—Fr. Jerome Cummings

Chapter 19
POWERLINE ASSERTIVENESS

*Y*our ability to be assertive can alter the quality of your life. Partners, occupations, friends, home environments, happiness and misery are all dependent upon your ability to stand up for yourself. The result of choosing to do so is higher self-esteem and self-awareness that will maximize your Line.

The power of finding your voice in the world is essential to overcoming the fears and failures that may plague your life. Before you can depend on yourself, you must find your voice. Years of intimidation have successfully silenced all of us, except for a few outspoken big-mouths. Since their vote in a relationship will typically be completely to their benefit, you may wake up one morning with a life that does not resemble any of your dreams.

To get back on the "road not yet traveled" by you, first set your goals bounded by your values, figure out the direction from your starting point to your goal, no matter how far, then ask repeatedly what your first step is, then the next step in that direction. Put a time limit on it or it will just hover in space. Do not view your journey as standing on one side of a great chasm, seeing the rim of other side as a futile impossibility to reach. Just take the first step in the series. Your task is merely to get from Point A to Point B; and if that means building bridges, catapults, or even airplanes to get to Point B, then that's where you set your sights—and map out your objectives.

MARY SCORES

Mary went to see SCORE, a group of retired executives that help new businesses. A group of elderly, white-haired men sat around a table listening intently while she described her financial and business situation. They told inside jokes, laughed a lot and delivered advice on how to build her practice as fast as Mary could write.

Mary had a goal (to survive), a direction (get more patients), and now she knew the first steps she could take (business cards, speaking engagements, attend all meetings around town and pass out cards).

Mary called all the organizations in town, offered to speak on stress to their groups, and passed out her business cards. She listened to business tapes in the car on how to improve her business practices. She said yes to every offer that would help build her business, even though she hated being away from her family, and despite the fact she was uncomfortable with public speaking—especially for free.

She did it anyway.

A year later, her income had gone up ten-fold.

Say "Yes," to whatever takes you in the direction of your goals bounded by your values. Be careful not to do anything bad in the name of getting somewhere good. The means must be as right for you as the ultimate end.

How many times have things looked pretty bad, but then out of nowhere a result happens that is better than you could have imagined? It might be luck or God, or your wonderful deceased mother intervening from another realm, who knows? We have no clue how any goal or project may end, so you cannot let the end justify anything you do wrong. In retrospect, the journey is often richer and more meaningful than achieving the goal. Make the decision to remain as conscientious in your journey as you are in selecting your goals. The medical dictum "first do no harm" could apply to everyone, not just doctors.

Knowing the right direction and taking the first step toward it are miles apart for some people. Sometimes our own fear and past failures incapacitate us, or we are simply intimidated by the scary unknown. The first step is the hardest—so make it small and easy.

FOCUS FACT FEELING FUTURE

Did someone push your mute button? Was it your parent's strict rules, a boyfriend's or girlfriend's control of you, your buddies' ridicule, or society's role for you that make you afraid to speak up? Learning **assertiveness** is mandatory because it makes life easier for everyone.

What is assertiveness? It is not being pushy, bossy or rude. Assertiveness is what allows your opinion to be heard so that you can take control of your half of your relationships. How you handle daily conflict can make or break your relationship.

People typically approach conflict in relationships by expressing themselves with one of the following ways:

- Aggression

- Assertiveness

- Passive-Aggressive Behavior

- Passivity/Depression

These four levels of communication can define your relationship—which of the four you use is up to you. The only one that can actually improve relationships is **Assertiveness.**

Aggression represents loud or threatening communication and behavior. Even a raised eyebrow can be threatening if you believe that person might (on purpose) lose control. Passive-aggressive behavior pretends to be innocent, but it is calculated. It is aggression gone underground, coupled with premeditated hostility, covered by a smile. "Oh, did you call me for dinner? I didn't hear you," is so harmless sounding, yet he or she *did* hear you. The motivation was to get to you, make you angry or win some competitive power-battle in your partner's mind.

Passivity/Depression is either letting someone walk all over you, or helplessly ceasing to care.

Good communication is **Assertive.**

Assertiveness is a sentence that starts with "I want..." or "I think..." or "I need..." and makes a truthful statement followed by a description of the action you intend to take.

Remember the concept of assertiveness in four words: **"Focus, Fact, Feeling, Future."** Choose one topic, state your facts and say how you feel about them. Then say exactly what you are planning to do about it.

PICKING YOUR BATTLES

The quickest way to become ineffective is to dilute your message.

Let us say, for instance, that your mission on a particular day is to have everybody's shoes picked up from the hallway—and not by you (again). You announce that desire to your family, and then you go on to demand that the kitchen counter be cleaned, the kids stop teasing the dog, and someone write the thank you cards from Christmas. Soon eyes glaze over and your message is not being heard. In fact, who can tell what you really want done? The result is probably shoes left in the hallway.

If you ask for multiple things all at once, you are definitely not going to get them, and then you start a pattern of failure. You are becoming a loser. People stop paying attention. Spreading your demands all over the map renders you powerless and ineffective.

Turn your situation around with the four F's: Focus-Fact-Feeling-Future, and become a winner.

WHAT MATTERS?

You must decide what is most important to you, right now. Focus on only one subject like no shoes in the hallway, create an annoying consequence that you can fulfill, and you will get results—because your family will discover that you are serious. They may not value the cleaned hallway or your comfort, but they will value avoiding your consequence.

Therein resides the secret, the *consequence!*

The important thing is that you establish a pattern of getting what you want and especially getting what you need. "When you ain't happy, ain't nobody happy."

Your mission in learning to be assertive is to create a long series of small successes, a habit of getting what you want, a pattern of power—a pattern observed and responded to by others. Remember, you have already trained people to treat you the way they do now.

Assertiveness is not meant to be selfishly misused against others, rather to bring equity—balance and fairness—back into your relationships when it is lacking. People need to get in the mode of taking what you want seriously, giving you what you want, and making you happy—at least fifty percent of the time. That is only fair.

When you ask for something big and important, like asking your teenager to not abuse alcohol or use drugs, you want to have established a pattern of power and respect for your authority long before then. You are very likely to get what you ask for if you have worked hard on assertiveness skills.

The following lesson will take you a long way. This particular lesson is not about shoes or clean hallways. It is about reestablishing *your* power and equalizing an out of balance relationship. Never use this to take advantage of innocent people. You need to use assertiveness with your family as a teaching tool, done with a tongue-in-cheek sense of humor to people you love, people who need to be seriously re-trained.

ASSERTIVENESS 101

1. Name Names

Whom are you addressing?

"Tom, I want your shoes put back in your closet every day."

Psychological field tests have shown that most people in a crowd will walk right past an actor pretending to have a heart attack, unless they are specifically identified by name or clothing.

2. The "I" Statement

"Tom, *I want* your shoes put back in your closet every day."

No one can argue with an "I" statement: it is your fact. "I want or I need or I feel or I..."

3. Action

"Tom, I want *your shoes put back in your closet* every day."

Can you describe like a photograph exactly what it is that you want?

Some experts say we think in mind-pictures. Our brain sees a picture of what you say. Negatives are very difficult for the mind to see. If you tell a child, "Don't slam the screen door!" the picture in his or her mind will be one of the door slamming and that is exactly what you will get because the "don't" is hard for the brain to register. If you speak in negatives you will get the opposite behavior more often than if you speak in clear pictures and eliminate a "don't" or a "no" laid on top. In fact, these kinds of words are impossible for children under ten to process quickly, and sometimes not at all. Turn all requests into a positive photograph and eliminate the negatives, as in, "Close the door quietly."

You are much more likely to get what you want when you word your request with positive words that create "a photograph in your mind of an action." A child can imagine what closing a door quietly looks like and can then do it.

Set people up to succeed.

Which statement gives the mind-picture that you want?

- "Clean up the house." (Nope. Too broad)

- "This hallway is looking really great!" (Sarcasm never works)

- "No shoes in the hallway." (Bad, bad. A negative over a mind-picture)

- "Put your shoes in your closet." (Good. A clear action picture)

4. Time

"Tom, I want your shoes put back in your closet *every day when you get home.*"

Specify exactly when you want something to happen as in "by five o'clock," or "before you leave for your dance lesson." Otherwise, your loved ones will postpone your "goofy" needs until they feel like doing it, which is never.

"Oh, did you mean this week?

5. Feeling

This is direct communication about why you want something as ridiculous as a clean hallway. Maybe you are concerned with **safety**. Maybe the shoes **stink**. Maybe they do not look nice and your **home's appearance is important** to you. Maybe everyone will start leaving his or her shoes there, even company, and the front door will not open. The use of the authoritarian parental one-upper line of, **"Just because I say so,"** is really not useful to teaching. Be sure to tell the truth in your explanation of why. This is an important assertiveness step even though no one may be listening. They are scrambling in their brains for their excuses to throw at you as soon as you stop talking.

6. Future—the "Or Else..."

This is the best! The **consequence**—believe me, you are dead without it. Do not bother starting if you do not have a small, and creative consequence planned that you have the power to deliver. You must give fair WARNING prior to imposing a consequence with time for people to consider the pros and cons. No "snake bite" and quick unfair reactions allowed. Slow down, and gently teach.

"Tom, I want your shoes in your closet every day or **else I am not cooking you dinner.**"

"Tom, I want your shoes in your closet every day or **else I won't be able to drive you to the party.**"

"Tom, I want your shoes in your closet every day or **else I am hiring a maid and deducting that from my share of the expenses.**"

Peer pressure works on family members, too. When everyone is waiting for dinner, point out the remaining shoes in the hallway, shake your head sadly and do not budge until your family removes the shoes to your satisfaction. The rest of the family will become allies to a clean hallway amazingly fast.

Be sure to start your consequences small, things that you do for others that will be inconvenient for them if suddenly missing, so you can carry it off and even escalate it, if necessary.

Irritating is exceedingly more effective then "mean."

7. Expect a Counterattack

Know that there will be a reaction from the family members equal to how unfair your relationships have become. People want to do what they want to, right now, and get angry if they do not get their way. They will act as if you are horrific when you do your little annoying consequence. However, you did not get what you wanted, so why should they? You are an equal to your partner and your children. If they do not care about your wants and needs, have no pity and take no prisoners. Win.

That is why you never ever give a consequence that you cannot enforce. Remember to do this with complete pity for the poor souls who did not listen to you. You are so sorry that they are inconvenienced at this point. You made yourself perfectly clear. It was their choice to ignore both you and your warning. Not your fault, but their fault.

Equity benefits all your relationships.

8. Feel Sorry for Them

Act like it hurts you more to deliver the consequence than the ones receiving the consequence. Show lots of pity for their failure to take heed, just be prepared to follow through completely with the consequence.

If you say that you want no shoes in the hallway, then chances of having shoes removed because people love you are very small unless you add that there will be a consequence affecting their comfort, their wealth or their pride. Never waiver, so make your consequences as small and annoying as possible to get the effect that you want. Make sure your consequence does not create a hardship on you. In fact, make the consequence something you do not want to do anyway, like housework or errands. A job that your trainee has imposed upon you is even more believable.

Begin with a small task that you want completed and stay focused on that task until your family knows you are quite serious. There is no need to give a big explanation.

Remember, to ask in an extremely pleasant way:

> "I would like the hallway cleaned and all shoes put away properly in your rooms, because I have friends coming over and I want the hallway clean. There are now shoes in the hallway. I would like those picked up in the next hour by everyone. Shoes that are not picked up will be confiscated and held for the next few days. You will have to make do without shoes, and I am not kidding."

Say these words firmly in a pleasant manner. Use no sarcasm. Sarcasm is a weak tool of the passive aggressive, not for an assertive person. Think "General" not "Sergeant." An order can be given in a whisper when you have the power and the influence to make it happen, think of Marlon Brando as the Godfather. If you do this in a very sweet voice, you will seem scary.

After an hour, if nothing happens, in a showy dramatic way, you get a trash bag, flop it noisily around in the air and begin to toss shoes in the trash bag. The family will scramble to retrieve shoes at this point and will have learned a valuable lesson—**you mean what you say.**

Let them have their shoes and say, "Wow, you were really cutting it close; you almost lost your shoes for three days," as if that would be a catastrophe.

If someone ignores you, no matter what, do not give up those shoes for three days (or whatever your consequence was), or you will be disregarded forever. The follow-through on the consequence cannot be overemphasized! That is where you win. In a shoe emergency, you can barter for your car washed in exchange for the urgently needed soccer shoes and you win again.

Do others believe that you mean what you say? This is critical to the success of your relationships. If you are met with a counterattack that frightens you, violence, destruction, hurtful words, then think about finding a new "family."

Even children can be temporarily emotionally fired if they are making you live in misery.

Once you begin to think about firing people who do not take you seriously, their power to intimidate you shrinks considerably. They will see you look at them with cold, fearless eyes. You will be surprised how fast people can change when you begin to act as if you are serious!

Trust equals: "Say what you mean," "Mean what you say," and that, "You will follow up with consequences."

Nothing you say has any power whatsoever unless there is a genuine, practical consequence. Would you always drive the speed limit without the threat of a ticket? Without the consequence, there is rarely compliance. Only when immediate direct reprisal for failure to grant your demands is forthcoming will you receive a direct response in defense of that consequence.

Ultimately, you will have no shoes in the hallway, more power-balanced relationships and a lot more of what you want.

EQUAL DIVISION OF WEALTH

The weaker partner tends to be absorbed into the lives of the stronger, more aggressive partner.

Are you over-socialized or dominated into subservience? Have you been programmed to give up your wants and desires in exchange for another's company? Are your partner's tastes now your tastes? If your partner is into drugs, alcohol or butterfly collecting, must you absorb his or her hobbies too?

If your own desires are less established, even people who care about you may overlook your interests.

BARBARA AND CALEB

Barbara wanted to spend time with her husband, Caleb, and she needed attention from him. Caleb was seriously into boating. He enjoyed going boating every weekend regardless of whether Barbara would join him or not. Therefore, in order to be with her man, Barbara found herself boating a lot.

Barbara loved classical music and wanted to learn to play the piano. Caleb had no interest in music, but did not mind if she went to a concert by herself. He, however, was going boating. Barbara wanted to be with Caleb so much that she slowly gave up all her interests so that she could accompany him.

Caleb loved having her join him, and told her so often. Caleb decided he needed a bigger boat. When he announced to Barbara that he had gone to some boat shows and had selected a new boat that he wanted to buy, she stormed out of the house. She was angry, but not really at poor bewildered Caleb.

As she passed a house, she heard someone practicing his or her scales on a piano and Barbara had a moment of clarity.

Caleb and Barbara had a limited amount of money to spend on entertainment. Caleb was about to take the majority of that money for something he wanted, with no consideration for her. If she did not object, he would buy that new boat tomorrow, and never even know why she was upset.

Not fair, it was her money, too. She decided that he would not purchase another boat until she had her piano. Caleb complained at first as he saw no need for a piano, yet he went with her to buy it.

Now some days Barbara stays home and practices her classical music. She lets Caleb know how happy that makes her when she greets him at the door smiling, too.

The stronger, more aggressive personalities will trudge right over you to get what they want. That is your fault for lying down on the floor and letting them.

If you just lie there like a doormat, **everyone** will walk all over you. The weaker partner must become stronger, to the point of balance and equity, or the relationship will become horribly imbalanced and the whole relationship system will fail. Will the strong-willed partner notice the inequity of the relationship and help the weaker one? No.

"We always deceive ourselves twice about the people we love—first to their advantage then to their disadvantage."

—**Albert Camus**

Chapter 20
LINE OF QUESTIONING

A "professional custody evaluation," performed in order to help determine custody of a child in a divorce proceeding, requires a determination as to the fitness of both parents to raise a child. A therapist gives a prediction to a judge, indicating which parent would be more inclined to provide for their child the necessary parenting elements, as well as not to alienate that child from the non-custodial parent.

It is torturous work at best.

THE INTAKE INTERVIEW

Imagine if within the first few minutes of the appointment, an evaluator believed every word one parent said, without talking to the other parent and many others, and made a snap judgment uncovering no other facts. How often would the evaluator be wrong—and with what dangerous consequences?

Yet many lonely people make similar snap judgments about the people they let into their hearts. Within minutes, we decide if we like someone. Sometimes our imagination allows our bodies to be excited and weak-kneed from little else than the way a person walks into a room. The sobering fact is that each encounter with a new partner holds the promise of "Magic," and if you are not careful, the potential for heartbreak, disease, or even violence.

How can we improve the odds of choosing correctly? What research will provide us with the answers? Does this person deserve another minute of our time? Is it safe to sleep with that one? Are you deluding yourself out of desperation? Matchlines Analysis will help you sail through a dangerous sea of emotions to find your relationship oasis.

CHECK IT OUT

When you see someone new, you size him or her up. You may rate confidence levels by posture or facial expressions. If he or she meets your eyes and smiles, you may award positive attributes to a complete stranger. If the stranger looks at you and does not return your smile, you may turn distrustful immediately.

Professional actors study these very specific behaviors, and then they duplicate the behaviors when they play parts: the bad person this week, the hero next week. However, the actors reveal their true self only in the choices that they make about the roles. Many fans may have completely misjudged the stars' ethics and values— good qualities might be sadly lacking in the rich and famous real lives.

Although we may be smug about the naïve young fan adoring movie star idols, we all compulsively create fantasies about every person we meet. It is crucial for survival instantly to distinguish friend from foe. In times that were more dangerous our snap judgments told us if we were looking at an enemy, if we were in danger and if we should flee or fight. Snap judgments are unfair, yet, instinctively essential to survive a sudden crisis.

How many times have you been crestfallen when a public servant, a teacher or a man of the cloth turns out to be a lying crook, or worse? You did not really know that person. Instead, you laid a persona on him or her of your own making, and then he or she disappointed you with real behavior.

In reality, we meet new people, and then bit by bit we form a judgment from what they say and do, and unfortunately, from what we need them to be. Sometimes a blank slate walks up and says "Hello," and suddenly, we throw a hologram blanket over his or her head declaring, "I have found the perfect one!"

Hold on, Sisters and Brothers!

We have to do a thorough **intake evaluation, which is a process not an event,** before we can make our judgment—or any semblance of an accurate, informed judgment.

Furthermore, this process of evaluation and judgment must remain in a liquid state for at least a year before it can harden into truly "knowing" a person. At what point do you begin to rely on your judgment of a new person? Even then, your odds of being right about another are still iffy.

How long does it really take to get to know someone? The average teen relationship, including courtship, physical relationship and break-up, comes to fruition in only a few months. In your twenties, you may sleep with someone too soon just to get to know him or her. Unfortunately, the new "friend" is often gone before you learn much else, other than physical information. By the time, you are in your late thirties and forties, being alone starts to sound better than painful heartbreak once again. If you found the perfect partner, time passes and you both have changed a little and need some balancing and fine-tuning. Some people think they can skip the intake interview completely because they can wing it.

JEREMY UNDER THE HOOD

Jeremy knows a lot about cars. He is the one that everyone calls when he or she is buying a new car. He is always under the hood, on his back under the car, and opening up panels that appear solid.

When Jeremy meets a new lady, and if she has the right look, he immediately describes her as "different" from other girls he has dated, "special," someone he could really get "serious about." However, he does not look under the hood or check the tires. He just buys the shiny paint. He has a fake, made-up image of her, one he creates in his own mind.

After daily marathon dating, who she really is begins to peek through. Then Jeremy dissolves into his own disappointment, proving once again to himself that he is unlucky in love and all women are the same. What he means by that is that she is not the idealized woman he wants her to be.

Now, this man really wants a good relationship with a good woman. Moreover, he would make a wonderful husband once he finally commits. Yet, for Jeremy, he cannot get past the first step of dating because he fails to perform an intake evaluation.

Jeremy's problem is that he gives each new woman all the positive points at the beginning—she is perfection. As their dating proceeds and he discovers that she is mere flesh and blood instead of perfection, he subtracts points. The poor girl rides the Madonna escalator to the top, and then she has nowhere to go except way back down to normal.

Many of Jeremy's new wonder-women try valiantly to live up to his vision of perfection however; they all eventually crash to earth. Stricken by reality, he runs away from ordinary selves. His partner's are devastated and so is he. Jeremy could stop this cycle of "romantic obscuring" if he only took time for an intake interview.

What Jeremy doesn't realize is that before he becomes enamored, if he could see what the pros and cons of the relationship would be, he might be pleasantly surprised, instead of always disappointed—and a girl might actually have a real chance with him.

How do you get information about another person before you get too involved? It is not that easy. The following example might help you to see the process. Let us walk through an ordinary conversation as two people meet.

An irresistibly cute girl smiles at you at the bar:

You: *Hey. May I buy you a drink?*

New Girl: *Yeah, thanks. Just orange juice, though.*

You: *That's a big bruise on your arm.*

New Girl: *My ex pushed me last night at midnight. My brother and I stopped by to get some stuff from the apartment. I had our baby in my arms. The guy is such a loser.*

New Girl is telling excessive information to a complete stranger. She wants you to feel sorry for her. She wants to talk about what others have done to her. You, however, want to know about her behavior. Your goal is to move the conversation back on the New Girl's behavior.

> **You:** *Why did you go back to the apartment so late at night?*
>
> **New Girl:** *He thought I wanted to see if the girl who was calling him all the time was there. I think she is a dealer or something. But, he thinks I still want him.*

If she is jealous of an ex, there may not be room for someone new in her life. If she is policing him, she may have good intentions, although she is way out of line. She may be a drama queen who stirs up trouble. Ask about her intention behind the action.

> **You:** *Did you really expect him to like that you were checking up on him?*
>
> **New Girl:** *I don't care. He's been partying ever since I moved out, and has not come to take the baby at all. He is never home, and we saw his lights on, and I needed her swing. Unless his mom comes by, I never get a break.*

Maybe she did have good intentions. Unfortunately, the ex sounds like a Loser. Lighten up the situation and return to serious questions intermittently

> **You:** *Let's drink to moms!*
>
> **New Girl:** **(Laughing)** *Let's not.*

Red Flag!

People often hide very strong statements under the veil of humor or laughter. What is the deal with her mom? Come back to this later.

You: *Can you make him be a good dad if he does not want to?*

New Girl: *Hey, he is the one who is really messing up here. He told me that he would help me raise the baby. He thinks that just because he goes off to work and pays for some stuff, that is enough. Then, he can do whatever he wants. But, I work hard, too. You know what? This is the first time I have been out for months.*

Maybe she is too bitter. Is she negative about all men?

You: *Do you think your ex acts the same as other guys his age?*

New Girl: *My friend Ursula's husband is twenty and he helps her all the time. They party a lot, too. Maybe that's what happened to us. I'm not going to waste my life with drugs and alcohol. I've seen too much of that. So, what do you do for a living?*

Red Flag!

New Girl is telling you that alcohol and drugs have been a problem in the past, and perhaps even with her mother. She is putting the conversation on you to cool off the hot topic. She did say something good about a man. She wants to assess if you are potential dating material. Always have a good answer to this question.

You: *I have been working in construction. I am studying to get my contractor's license. I always wanted to be an architect. Just need time and money. (Back on her.) What do you want to do after your daughter goes to school?*

New Girl: *I haven't even thought about that for a while. Oh, I wanted to have a French Bakery. Or, maybe a coffee shop with atmosphere and good jazz at night. I always wanted to be a stay home mom, too, but you never get to talk to anyone. It's just really hard by yourself with a child.*

I love her so much. Compared to my friends, I don't even have a life anymore. I never go out, and I have to take Jenny with me everywhere. I just don't think I can do it on my own with no help.

New Girl is showing some desperation here. She is still looking for sympathy albeit well deserved. Does she like you, or does she like what you can potentially do for her? Try the mother question again.

You: *Does your mother help you with Jenny?*

New Girl: *No. I don't let her take the baby. She was never there for me.*

Okay. What information can we extract from these first few minutes?

Negatives: Definite problems with the mother. Definite issues with drinking and drugs. Maybe her mother has a drinking problem. The presence of alcohol can often precede neglect, abuse and even molestation. New Girl reports only that her mother neglected her. There will be more. If New Girl has a fear of abandonment, then she may have put a strangle hold on her Ex. If she were a victim of abuse, then she may have gone back to their apartment looking for a fight because that is her manifestation of love—as she knows it.

She knew her Ex was partying and that he may have been drinking. Nevertheless, she put herself and their baby at risk by her timing. Did she want to catch him with another woman? Alternatively, is she self-destructive? We need to know if we are dealing with abandonment, abuse, neglect or exaggeration.

What is clear, at least from her perspective, is that she has a negative Ex. The Ex is apparently not someone that you would enjoy interacting with on a weekly or daily basis if you became a stepparent. She feels burdened with a baby and has a small support group. She is frustrated and somewhat desperate. New Girl has a Compressed Line. She could even have a Faultline if the issues about her mother are childhood ones.

Positives: She is not a drinker. She likes coffee and jazz as perhaps you do, and maybe she can bake. She is trying to be a good mother. She is open, maybe too open, enjoys talking and being social. The Line-compression resulting from caring for a young child is temporary.

Would you ask a girl like this out?

Your Love Actions

No matter how much you love your partner, if what you do does not match his or her love definition, then your partner can only conclude that you do not love him or her. If you are love-speaking to your partner in a way that makes you happy, yet infuriates him or her, what have you accomplished? For example, if your partner speaks only Spanish and you say, "I love you," in Swedish, then you do not get very far.

You see, each of us hears the same sentence differently with different inflection, emphasis and hidden meanings. The length of a Relationship Capacity Line is represented by *deeds* more than words. Words are too easy. A new lover can tell you right now that he or she loves you more than anyone in the world does. That costs nothing to say. Do you think that same person will be there at your side helping you if you are ill or sad? Promises and words do not demonstrate commitment. Actions do. Words do not count much. Therefore, when you use Matchline Analysis, try to use only actions for assessing and scoring your relationships.

Sometimes a spouse, a lover or a parent *really wants* to be there for you, but jobs, reality, or a more urgent commitment forces them to put you second. That is understandable and not a big deal occasionally. Missing a ballet recital because you have to work is very different than missing the performance because you are hanging around after work having a beer with the boys.

Fortunately, living a lie is more difficult than one might expect. People invariably slip up and the truth shines through their behavior. Desperate-for-love people will write off these moments of truth and clarity with excuses.

BRITNEY BELIEVES

Brittney was a great artist, and she earned herself a free ride to the University. Shy and introverted, Brittney did not date except for a handful of casual dates with friends.

In her junior year, her art teacher began to make advances. She knew her teacher had feelings for her—he was older, and she asked him to stop pursuing her. However, he was persistent. The teacher had mentored her, shared her exhibitions and awards and spent her best times with her for the past three years. He was a little skinny, changed plans a lot, and sometimes very pushy. In spite of the fact that he was her teacher, he was so easy to talk to and fun, that she let herself fall in love.

He often had to work or cancelled their dates, yet never had a girl been so gently wooed. He said he would join her when she moved after graduation, but something always came up.

They planned their wedding, even though he still had not moved to her city. He gave her an engagement ring, and she even put a down payment on a condominium. However, a month before the wedding Brittney's Uncle Nick, who worked for the police force, ran a background check just to be sure.

Well, what d'ya know? Did the teacher's lovely existing wife and two children just slip his mind? Was he going to go through with the second wedding as a bigamist, or simply leave Brittney crying at the alter?

Brittney was indeed rescued by her loving uncle, however she felt like she had been run over with the betrayal and loss. She believed her teacher's words, when the evidence was telling her something else entirely.

If you are making excuses for your beloved's behavior, watch out. Rats cannot get away with their deceptions unless someone plays the patsy.

Are you blaming the rat?

Holding on to anger and thoughts of revenge over a love gone wrong will render you immobile. When you finally accept the fact that you may have done the hurting to yourself, and that you are currently still mistreating yourself by flooding your body with poisonous anger, then the sooner you can free up a crate of emotional baggage.

In your next healthy, happy relationship, you will count only **observed behavior,** not easy words. When you are assessing your partner in the Matchline Quizzes or in your daily life, score only actions and truth that you observe first-hand or behavior that has been confirmed by several sources.

Part 6

FINISH LINE

"*To love someone deeply gives you strength. Being loved by someone deeply gives you courage.*"

—Lao Tzu

Chapter 21
YOU HAVE A FINE LINE

*M*atchlines for Singles has revealed several tools that can help you to balance tumultuous relationships. You probably now know more than you ever wanted to know about your parents' relationship. You may have even fine-tuned your interactive skills. If so, then you have learned to take baby steps...while preparing for the backlash of resistance from family and friends. Perhaps you even know yourself a little better. How will you apply the skills that you have learned? Have you ever imagined relationships in other ways?

MEMBER OF PLANET EARTH

You also have quite a large relationship with the Planet, the world in which we all live and love. How you act in this unique relationship can have an important impact on the lives of your children and grandchildren for generations. Do you fulfill certain societal obligations to clean up your own messes in your yard or factory, to share with others, and to notice when a part of your world around you is hurting and do what you can to help? On the other hand, do you act like a Bottomline in your relationship to Earth and her inhabitants?

What is your relationship with your country? Do you see only its good qualities and look the other way when it misbehaves, ignoring its faults?

What is your relationship with your own neighborhood? Do you hope that when you are old and perhaps alone that some kind neighbor stops by for a chat? If so, then have you ever done that for the elderly, or for the handicapped, or that kid that got in trouble down the street?

Did you list any of the following items as your personal goals or values?

- Your Health

- Your Family's Health

- Your Children as a Priority

- Peace of Mind

- Safety

- Clean World, Food, and Water

- Honesty and Integrity

- Sacrificing Now for a Peaceful and Secure Future

Think of each of these virtues in the big picture, from a global perspective right down to your own neighborhood. How do you choose to apply a global perspective to your everyday actions? Has our world ever been so interconnected and dependent on each other's behavior? What relationship do you want our world leaders to have with each other-a healthy assertive and balanced relationship or an abusive aggressive hate-creating one?

FREE TO BE

You are more than just an individual; you have history! Your DNA goes back to the first people on earth. You have a connection with all the people who have ever lived and strived from the beginning of human history. You can add self-esteem by the ton to whatever you have accomplished in your own life if you think of yourself as a link in a wonderful chain.

Allow yourself to open your memory to a relationship with the people who have died to win us our freedom from old enemies that we now call our friends, from prejudice, chauvinism, religious intolerance, serfdom, slavery— the list goes on back through history. They were heroes (and heroines) so we do not have to be. Yet, maybe we can be a hero or a heroine in a way, if we make all our relationships a little better. The trickle-up effect works!

Just remember, you have a total right and opportunity to be eccentric and different within the small space in time that we call our lives, because of others who cared and did something. You have just as much right to exist, vote, laugh and feel love as does any great self-appointed royalty. Each time that you protect your freedom to be you, then you also protect all people who desire freedom. You cannot predict how or when your small act of kindness, compassion or courage might change the world. The outcome will be determined perhaps without you ever knowing. A big self-esteem boost might be your surprise benefit.

Also, ask yourself if your enjoyment of freedom impinges on anyone else in a way that he or she can no longer be free. Greed has paid for much abuse around the world. If someone tries to deny you the freedom to design your life as you see fit, then you must fight loudly with your voice, your vote, your money, and your work to protect the right to live your special life assertively—in both your intimate relationships as well as in your larger societal relationships. Pretend the heroes and heroines of yesterday are watching.

WHERE DO I START?

Are you in a group? Are you a member of an association?

If so, try to remain slightly separated from your groups, parties and associations and remain first an individual, who may differ from all the regulations of membership and conformity required just to "belong." Start small to raise the awareness of how you affect your planet-relationship, or you may feel overwhelmed. Seriously consider talking to that old neighbor or rascal kid down the street. If we dare try, we might just change the world in infinite ways.

Slowly, every day, our "normal" environment is continually changing. Power shifts from one to another, people die, the young invent and rules change. Will your voice be heard, or will you let the less qualified choose what is best for you and your planet? Be different and be heard.

In Gratitude

To the thousands of patients who for over a span of two decades entrusted me with their mental well-being, relationships, families and friends, thank you. Their triumphs and their tragedies—many of which have left us giggling together or tearful during therapy sessions—have taught us many powerful and important lessons on the absurdity of life, fully believing the maxim: **"You always get caught,"** and **the first rule of happiness is to "Stop lying."**

Matchlines for Singles is not intended to be a reflection of a perfect life or any form of personal therapy, rather a theory of relationships based on education, experiences and research. Please rely on a good professional therapist who can address your problems personally. I have endeavored to generalize in this book in order to teach, rather than to try to give individual therapy.

Our lives all have a fair share of fits and starts, failures and successes, a measure of joy, tears, mistakes, and both good times and bad. Try to laugh through most days, knowing from experience that grief never stays for long, and keep hopeful, believing that somehow things will work out all right. They usually do.

Do what you know is right. Strive to keep your actions kind, moral and ethical to ensure success. Whoever you are or want to be, may you have great success on your journey, and a lifetime of good relationships with many Matchlines who share your joys and lighten your sorrows.

"Now join your hands, and with your hands your hearts."

—William Shakespeare

♥

Wishing you love and peace.

Dr. Molly Barrow holds a Ph.D. in clinical psychology and is an authority and speaker on psychological topics, including relationships, self-esteem, and parenting. She is a member of the American Psychological Association, Screen Actors Guild, and Authors Guild and is a licensed mental health counselor for children, adolescents and adults.

Dr. Molly has appeared as an expert in film, teen documentaries, KTLA Impact, NBC news, PBS, and WBZT talk radio. She is quoted in O Magazine, Psychology Today, Newsday, Oprah.com, CNN.com, eslteacherboard.com, Parenting Blog, AIA.org, Newlyweds.com, The Nest, MSN.com, Yahoo, Match.com, Women's Health, Super Vision, Harvard Business School, Women's World and the New York Times. Listen to Dr. Barrow's radio show on blogtalkradio.com and read her column at Menstuff.org. Please visit Dr. Barrow's Official Web Site: http://www.drmollybarrow.com. The Matchlines Quizzes for Singles and Couples is based on 25 years of academic research, relationship therapy and family counseling. Selected as the Sunshine State Young Readers Award nominees, Dr. Barrow's self-esteem building, adventure books for children, *Malia and Teacup Awesome African Adventure* and *Malia and Teacup Out on a Limb,* may be found at http://www.MaliaandTeacup.com.

TAKE THE QUIZ

GO TO
WWW.DRMOLLYBARROW.COM
AND TAKE THE MATCHLINES QUIZ.

❤

ALL YOUR QUESTIONS REGARDING PAST
RELATIONSHIPS AND CURRENT ONES WILL BE ANSWERED.

❤

YOU WILL RECEIVE A PRINTED GRAPH SHOWING
YOU WHY YOUR PAST RLEATIONSHIPS DIDN'T WORK
AND . . . WHAT TO WATCH OUT FOR IN
FUTURE RELATIONSHIPS
YOU WILL SEE HOW TO AVOID MISMATCHES
AND HOW TO SELECT GREAT PARTNERS.

SAMPLE GRAPH

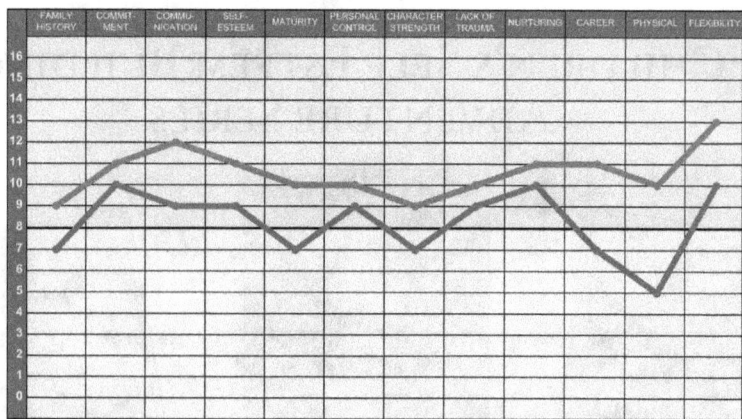

An analysis of each plotted point and your line, will accompany your personal graph which will explain everything you need to know about your current and/or next relationship and what your next move is.

COUPLES

TAKE THE COUPLES QUIZ AND LEARN WHERE
YOUR TROUBLE SPOTS ARE AND HOW TO FIX THEM.
WWW.DRMOLLYBARROW.COM

O Magazine

"Molly Barrow, PhD, a psychotherapist and author of Matchlines...was right, after all. She makes me feel better." O Magazine, Lisa Belkin, *Stop Nagging!*

Psychology Today Magazine

"If you ignore your partner's signals to back off, you're effectively being inconsiderate, not loving, warns Molly Barrow, author of Matchlines...Backing off is best, not only because it's respectful, but also because your partner will be more likely to then reach out to you." Jessica Dulong, *How Can I Keep From Suffocating in A Relationship*

About.com

"Barrow's top tips in key areas...With patience and diligence, you'll improve." Francesca Di Meglio

Boca News

"Having trouble with your love life? Always hooking up with the wrong guy? Matchlines has been written up in O Magazine and Psychology Today...a revolutionary new way of looking at relationships and making the right choices in love. I liked the book for two reasons. First, because the basic premise underlying her self-help techniques does not place blame. The second reason I liked the book is because the ideas and techniques are accessible...written in simple straight forward style, easy to understand and hopefully utilize the information the book contains." Prudy Taylor Board

Women's Health Magazine

"But affectionate surprises aren't just about take-me-now urges, says Molly Barrow, Ph.D. a psychotherapist and author of Matchlines. Barrow says 'That ideal is hardwired in our brains when we are looking for a mate.' Why? Because we seek out the best possible genetic material to pass on to our offspring." Kristina Grish, *What Turns You On?*

Sun Times Newspaper

"Dr. Molly Barrow's experience in front of and behind the camera helps her communicate and inform, whether as a teacher, guest speaker, contributor to documentary video projects, or expert witness. Now, growing out of her clinical work, Dr. Barrow has written—Matchlines." Philip K. Jason, columnist

Book of the Week
"Matchlines is the BOOK OF THE WEEK!" MENSTUFF.org

❤️

Virtual Private Library Outstanding Resource
"This is a truly an excellent book and true resource! This book describes and then gives you the tools that are necessary to discover the real you when it comes to understanding who is the best match for you! A must read for anyone truly interested in seeking the most appropriate match." Marcus P. Zillman, M.S

❤️

A Welcome Alternative to Dr. Phil
"Dr. Barrow...provides effective answers to questions affecting the myriad relationships that exist between couples, individuals, families and also businesses to assist in improving their communication skills, which is likely to improve those relationships. Dr. Barrow's open and approachable style to sharing knowledge is a welcome alternative for those who may be tiring of Dr. Phil's smirking 'how's that working for you?' approach to dealing with life's emotional challenges." iGoBlogtalk

❤️

The Unconscious Actor
"The unique, innovative formula will help you solve your problems. I learned a lot." Darryl Hickman, actor/author

❤️

Hodges University
"We will benefit from Dr. Barrow's wealth of information and enthusiasm." Dr. Elsa Rodgers

❤️

This is a self-help page-turner!
Matchlines is the first self-help page turner, I couldn't put it down. I learned more from this book than any other relationship self-help I have ever read. It will not only change the way you look at your relationships, it will change your life. I highly recommend it. Dr. Barrow should be hailed as a leader in her field. The Matchline theory is a very important discovery and one that all should experience and practice." Jeff Schlesinger, Publisher

Well Done

"You have categorized and presented them so that we can make sensible and productive real life decisions." Ed Machek, producer

♥

Mayor of Hollywood Master of Ceremonies, Hollywood Walk of Fame

"Dr. Molly Barrow's new book Matchlines contains an astonishing formula for solving love problems. Maybe it's time we turn the world's problems over to the good doctor! I'm sure she would have some cultured ideas on World Peace. Next stop—Tinseltown!" Johnny Grant, Ceremonial Mayor of Hollywood, *Posthumously*

♥

A Primer for Achieving Successful Relationships

"Dr. Molly provides simple to grasp concepts for understanding and coping with the complexities of contemporary American relationships. A truly worthwhile read for those who may or may not suffer from emotional tunnel vision but are seeking to better understand a potential mate while not having to compromise self-esteem." Anonymous

♥

Highly recommended!!!!

"I am looking for a wife. Matchlines taught me that I was looking in the wrong places and at the wrong type of person. Now I know what I need to make me happy. I recommend this book highly." Scott S. Boat Captain

♥

A Direct and Informative Book on Relationships

"Molly Barrow's new publication sheds a good deal of light on marriage and commitment. It is a must read and an important reference for those who want to be refreshed as to why they got married in the first place." Paul Slater

♥

A fresh and helpful perspective

"With her exceptionally well-expressed and original ideas, the author offers amazing insight and understanding of relationship dynamics. How you view and assess relationships will be changed forever! Anyone experiencing relationship turmoil as well as all relationship counselors will benefit from reading and hanging on to this book." Foster Reznor, Advertising Executive

A Return To Real Love

"The innocence and purity of love has once again entered my life. It is not possible to share how many times I had been with the wrong person. Beauty is candy for the eye but more often than not, a charade for the heart. It was a pleasure to follow this author's advice and in the end receive the gift of happiness." Nicholas Petrucci, Portrait Artist

It is a good book

"I think that in the market of relationship books it is difficult to choose. I would choose this over most of the books on the subject. The technique used is one that isn't in every other book on relationships. If you are feeling like there are areas your marriage could improve this would be a good read. Overall the writing is almost storylike which helps to make the concepts and techniques more realistic for the typical person who needs help. I can't stand when a book proposes great ideas that don't work. This is an plan that can work for everyone who actually cares about changing and not just having their ego stroked. The material is on point and it delivers what it promises. I hope this helped you in deciding. God Bless." Atom McCree, Marketing Director

How Does She Know My Life?

"How did she know exactly how and why my marriage failed? Her description is so spot on it's hard to believe she did not even know me. Her insights are astounding, and oh, so helpful in my present, and nearly perfect, relationship with another Longline." Connie Bransilver, Nature Photographer

Got me a husband

"This book helped me find the most wonderful and kindest man I have ever met. I had to look on the inside for a long love line and Dr. Molly's book showed me how to find him. Now I am married to him." Debbie

For Men Too!

"My husband, in-laws and I attended one of Dr Molly's seminars, and were intrigued by her theories about relationships. After purchasing her book, all of us have been reading this book. I was pleasantly surprised when my father in law - a man married for 46 years - mentioned how much he enjoyed this book. He finished it in record time, and found the book relevant, interesting, and informative. He said its one he will pass along to other couples. To me, this spoke volumes about this book." Katie Koestner, Attorney

Molly Barrow Rocks the Relationship World

"Molly Barrow has spent the last twenty years as one of Florida's busiest relationship therapists. She knows her stuff and she pours a great deal of extremely useful information and insight into her new book, Matchlines, which will do for relationships what Betty Crocker does for cake mix. Molly is a very spiritual person and her ideas and observations are not a bunch of scientific thought and charts and graphs. Matchlines offers up a very humanistic response to finding love in all the right places and I believe that she would put on a far more interesting show than Dr. Phil and Oprah. I was excited to read her book because of her reputation in the southeast and I wasn't in the least bit disappointed. I highly recommend this book to anyone who is trying to get their love life back on track." Steve Rubin, Motion Picture Producer Los Angeles

Tremendous Help

"The author takes the complicated subject of relationships and makes it understandable." David Edel, Banker

A "must read" for couples in all stages of relationships!

Right to the heart secrets of relationships.

"I've been married for 17 years and know a few things about relationships (being in a pretty good one) but then I read a pre-release copy of Dr. Molly's Matchlines, and holy cow, did I learn a lot. Revealing, insightful, and surprisingly accurate, the book gave me new ways of looking at all my relationships past and present. It showed me what I'm going right and wrong and suggestions for improvement. I can see the benefits in my relationship with my wife -- fun, new, and at times painfully honest, but all welcome. Good book." Eric Adams, Director

Brilliant.

"An inspiring and exceptional book I will refer to for guidance the rest of my life. I recommend it to everyone." Lola Barrow, American Embassy, D.R

A "must read" for couples in all stages of relationships!

Clear, easy to read, easy to find out about your future with the one you love.

Single, engaged or married- this book helps!

"I am happily married, but reading this book helped me understand why past relationships failed, and why this one works so well. It also helps me see the 'shorter lines' and 'longer lines' in my business relationships, and understand that MatchLines are there too." Suzie, reader of every relationship book

💜

Really helped our marriage

"Fast informative read funny illustrations good self help for men as well as the ladies. Have recommended it to friends."

💜

Outstanding Resource . . .

"This is a truly an excellent book and true resource! This book describes and then gives you the tools that are necessary to discover the real you when it comes to understanding who is the best match for you! A must read for anyone truly interested in seeking the most appropriate match . . ."

💜

This is a self-help page turner! ★★★★★ Rating

"Matchlines is the first self-help page turner, I couldn't put it down. I learned more from this book than any other 'relationship' self-help I have ever read. It will not only change the way you look at your relationships, it will change your life. I highly recommend it. Dr. Barrow should be hailed as a leader in her field. The 'Matchline' theory is a very important discovery and one that all should experience and practice."

💜

"Are you looking for a long-term love relationship with a short-term partner? If you are, you're in trouble. You need Dr. Molly Barrow's new book, "Matchlines." The unique, innovative formula she describes will help you solve your problems. I learned a lot from Dr. Molly's fascinating book, and I think you will, too." Darryl Hickman – Los Angeles actor, writer, director, producer, teacher and author of *The Unconscious Actor: Out of Control, In Full Command*

💜

Great Book. ★★★★★ Rating

"I have just finished reading this book and it helped me find a type of person that would be perfect for me. I recommended this book to some of my friends and they also found it very helpful."